Praise for *Becoming Sage*

We have so often focused our attention on millennials and the church while failing to attend to the significant realities surrounding discipleship in midlife. In this gem of a book, Michelle Van Loon issues an important wake-up call to the church to cultivate and support lifelong discipleship as she invites us to consider the particular issues being navigated by those in midlife. A powerful antidote to formulaic and quick-fix discipleship, *Becoming Sage* is a must-read for all in ministry and all in midlife as it calls us to nourish slow-growth disciples who can bear fruit in each season of life.

KRISTEN DEEDE JOHNSON
Dean and Vice President of Academic Affairs; professor of Theology and Christian Formation, Western Theological Seminary, Holland, MI

I'm old, depending on who's counting, so *Becoming Sage* spoke to me. Michelle Van Loon parses the realities of these years—spiritual, emotional, physical, and social. As Michelle points out, most of us are much more familiar with the stages of the first half of life than the last. Especially interesting was her insight into how our walk with Christ naturally changes and how we can leverage this season for maximum wisdom and influence—how we can become sage and not just old.

LEE ECLOV
Pastor and author of *Feels Like Home: How Rediscovering the Church as Family Changes Everything*

Becoming Sage is a gift to people of faith in midlife, that disorienting "time of reckoning" that Michelle Van Loon so deftly describes. We are encouraged to continue on as she reminds us that maturity is not a destination, but a process that doesn't follow a "tidy trajectory." Humorous, honest, and wise, Michelle is just the guide many of us need as we move through the second half of life. The prompts for reflection at the end of every chapter are much more nuanced and helpful than the norm. I look forward to journaling through each one.

JENNIFER GRANT
Author of *When Did Everybody Else Get So Old?: Indignities, Compromises, and the Unexpected Grace of Midlife* and *Maybe God Is Like That Too*

In light of almost one third of the population moving into midlife, the church needs guidelines as to how to move on to maturity and to not waste what can be, by God's grace, the most impactful and effective season of our life in advancing the kingdom of God. Michelle Van Loon has provided much-needed wisdom as to how to maneuver through the second half of life.

NANCY J. KANE
Author of *Stages of the Soul: God's Invitation to Greater Wisdom* and coauthor of *From Fear to Love: Overcoming Obstacles to Healthy Relationships*

Becoming Sage is for all of us who are famished, who long for sense amid so much "Christian" nonsense. In this book, Michelle Van Loon reveals just how sage she is. And if we heed her wisdom, it will rub off on us. I want to stick this book into the hands of every pastor, church leader, and seminary professor. It's that valuable. Apprentice yourself to Michelle's God-given wisdom; I have.

MARLENA GRAVES
Author of the forthcoming *The Way Up Is Down*

Most of us hope to grow wise as we grow old. But merely acquiring more biblical information or attending more church gatherings doesn't automatically lead to wisdom. In *Becoming Sage*, Michelle has given us reliable guidance for the journey of maturing in our life with God. In it, she provides a vision for a lifetime of transformation.

GEM AND ALAN FADLING
Founders of Unhurried Living and authors of *What Does Your Soul Love?: Eight Questions That Reveal God's Work in You*

Midlife can be a confusing and disorienting period. Too many enter these years unprepared, resulting in painful wandering or stalled maturity. Michelle Van Loon argues that it doesn't have to be this way. She has thought much and thought well about midlife. Michelle writes as a sage—a trustworthy guide through this vital stage.

ERIC SCHUMACHER
Coauthor of *Worthy: Celebrating the Value of Women*

There are so many opportunities to pursue in midlife. One is the invitation to become sage—spiritually and emotionally mature—intentionally drawing closer to God and His ways. If that's something you long for, this book will help you get there.

JILL SAVAGE
Author of *Empty Nest, Full Life: Discovering God's Best for Your Next*

As our churches focus on youth, studies show there's a quiet mass exodus of midlifer's out the back door. What are we missing? Michelle Van Loon shows us. With her characteristic brilliance and insight, she unpacks this little-known movement, then guides us—and the church—on a solid path toward the wisdom and spiritual maturity God calls all of us to. I personally feel freed from the twin evils of chasing youth and fearing old age. Instead, I'm aiming to "become sage."

LESLIE LEYLAND FIELDS
Author of *Your Story Matters: Finding, Writing and Living the Truth of Your Life*

When empty nest and job transition and location change all collided, I looked for a wise voice to guide me forward and came up short. *Becoming Sage* is exactly what I was looking for. With Michelle Van Loon as our seasoned guide, this book needs to be in the hands of everyone at midlife and beyond.

ANITA LUSTREA
Host of *Faith Conversations* podcast, spiritual director, media coach

Michelle Van Loon introduces us to a veritable "who's who" as she winds her way through the gifts and realities of becoming a sage. Drawing upon earthy biblical characters; wise, modern guides; as well as her own personal journey, she gives hope, vision, and purpose to this culminating season. You will feel that you are "surrounded by a great cloud of witnesses" who not only see you but also understand you as you move irresistibly toward the full flowering of your one, particular life.

DAVID BOORAM
Coauthor of *When Faith Becomes Sight: Opening Your Eyes to God's Presence All Around You*
Director of Fall Creek Abbey

In this wise and welcome field guide, Michelle Van Loon casts a vision for what our lives might look like if we refuse to settle and instead use the many challenges, losses, and disappointments of midlife as traction to keep growing. *Becoming Sage* not only empowers us to flourish today—it infuses us with hope for our future.

DOROTHY LITTELL GRECO
Author of *Making Marriage Beautiful: Lifelong Love, Joy, and Intimacy Start with You* and the forthcoming *Marriage in the Middle*

BECOMING SAGE

Cultivating Meaning, Purpose, and Spirituality in Midlife

Michelle Van Loon

MOODY PUBLISHERS

CHICAGO

All Scripture quotations, unless otherwise indicated, are taken from the Holy Bible, New International Version®, NIV®. Copyright © 1973, 1978, 1984, 2011 by Biblica, Inc.™ Used by permission of Zondervan. All rights reserved worldwide. www.zondervan.com. The "NIV" and "New International Version" are trademarks registered in the United States Patent and Trademark Office by Biblica, Inc.™

Scripture quotations marked NLT are taken from the Holy Bible, New Living Translation, copyright ©1996, 2004, 2015 by Tyndale House Foundation. Used by permission of Tyndale House Publishers, Inc., Carol Stream, Illinois 60188. All rights reserved.

Scripture quotations marked MSG are from The Message, copyright © 1993, 2002, 2018 by Eugene H. Peterson. Used by permission of NavPress. All rights reserved. Represented by Tyndale House Publishers, Inc.

Scripture quotations marked KJV are taken from the King James Version.

All emphasis in Scripture has been added.

Names and details of some stories have been changed to protect the privacy of individuals if any names or details have been modified in the book. Names marked by an * are composites drawn from a number of stories people shared with the author throughout the years.

The first section of chapter 9 was first published as "One Size Fits All Is a Fable" on ThePerennialGen .com, a blog collective cofounded by the author. Small portions of the book are adapted from articles the author has written for ChristianityToday.com. Used with permission.

Published in association with the literary agency of The Steve Laube Agency.

Edited by Amanda Cleary Eastep
Interior and cover design: Erik M. Peterson
Cover illustration of plants copyright © 2019 by Popmarleo / Shutterstock (271228691). All rights reserved.

Author photo: Gini Lange Images

Library of Congress Cataloging-in-Publication Data

Names: Van Loon, Michelle, author.
Title: Becoming sage : cultivating meaning, purpose, and spirituality in midlife / Michelle Van Loon.
Description: Chicago, IL : Moody Publishers, 2020. | Includes bibliographical references. | Summary: "There is no age restriction on spiritual growth. So, why do we act like there is? For the last several decades, Western churches have focused the bulk of their resources on the early stages of discipleship—children's Sunday school, youth group, college ministry. These are all important, but we've neglected spiritual growth in the second half of life. In fact, an outside observer might think that after the growth of the college years, the goal is simply to coast through the rest of your Christian life. Michelle Van Loon has a different idea. In Becoming Sage, she challenges those in midlife and beyond to continue to pursue radical spiritual growth, and she'll help you get started. She explores what the unique challenges of midlife can teach us about Jesus and how to think about everything from church, friends, and family, to money, bodies, and meaning. Don't settle for a life of coasting. Revitalize your spiritual growth, today"-- Provided by publisher.
Identifiers: LCCN 2019047009 | ISBN 9780802419446 (paperback) | ISBN 9780802498038 (ebook)
Subjects: LCSH: Middle-aged persons--Religious life. | Spiritual formation. | Older Christians--Religious life. | Aging--Religious aspects--Christianity.
Classification: LCC BV4579.5 .V365 2020 | DDC 248.8/4--dc23
LC record available at https://lccn.loc.gov/2019047009

Originally delivered by fleets of horse-drawn wagons, the affordable paperbacks from D. L. Moody's publishing house resourced the church and served everyday people. Now, after more than 125 years of publishing and ministry, Moody Publishers' mission remains the same—even if our delivery systems have changed a bit. For more information on other books (and resources) created from a biblical perspective, go to: www.moodypublishers.com or write to:

Moody Publishers
820 N. LaSalle Boulevard
Chicago, IL 60610

1 3 5 7 9 10 8 6 4 2

Printed in the United States of America

CONTENTS

INTRODUCTION

Someone at church told my boyfriend he thought I was the pinnacle of immaturity.

I was nineteen at the time. I was convinced the opposite was true of me, which might be your first clue that I wasn't at all mature. I figured I was all grown up by virtue of the fact that I was about to co-sign a lease on my first apartment with two of my high school pals. Of course, my idea of adulthood included being able to eat Oreos and cold pizza for breakfast, drive my aging Ford Maverick aimlessly around darkened Chicago suburban streets at 2 a.m., and follow Jesus without having to sneak around to do so. After spending most of my high school years forbidden by my unbelieving parents to attend church, the most important thing adulthood represented to me was the freedom to serve Jesus.

In the four decades since, I've eaten Oreos for breakfast on more than one occasion. I've driven around at 2 a.m. a few times,

I've discovered that maturity is not a destination, but an ongoing process.

usually in an attempt to lull a newborn to sleep. Despite the warning he received from a well-meaning church member, my boyfriend still asked me to marry him. We've been married four decades. And I'm still following Jesus.

Like many kids, I imagined adulthood was a goal and maturity was a given. But now that I've been adulting for a while, I've discovered that maturity is not a destination, but an ongoing process.

However, the process is not automatic. Some people plateau in their emotional, moral, and spiritual growth. This might be because of trauma, grief, abuse, or illness that happened at an earlier point in their lives. Or they've stalled because they've bought our culture's message that youth is the treasure they should spend their lives seeking. A deep need for security tethers others in place.

The word used in the New Testament for maturity is *teleios*,[1] a common word that means finished, complete, or fully grown. It describes the purpose of a Jesus follower's journey with Him. It is not the name of its destination.[2]

Midlife can be a time of reckoning, healing, and recalibration on the teleios road. This period of our lives can fuel meaningful change as God prunes lopsided growth and fruitless affections from our lives. God can use the "second adulthood" of our lives to deflate the ambition and hubris of our youth. It is a life stage that calls us to simultaneously leave behind and build on the past while pressing onward toward teleios (Phil. 3:12–15).

Midlife holds for each one of us the invitation to become sage—a way of life in which a person expresses experience, knowledge, insight, and self-mastery. That invitation to grow in wisdom can be well-disguised in the often-disorienting shifts that characterize this life stage.

In Scripture, one thing that set young Solomon apart from most other rulers was the one thing he asked of God upon becoming king: he asked for wisdom (1 Kings 3:9). We remember him because he didn't choose to ask for the usual things that an immature young person might ask for upon stepping into adult responsibilities—things like an impressive army dressed in spiffy uniforms, a giant pile of loot, or Oreos for breakfast. Over time, Solomon's vast wealth, power, and enormous harem of wives and concubines disconnected him from the Source and Giver of wisdom, and he grew more foolish as he aged (1 Kings 11:1–6).

We take the first step in becoming sage by recognizing how essential wisdom is to us.

But that is not how wisdom is meant to work. Throughout the Proverbs attributed to him, Solomon celebrates the priority of continually growing in wisdom over a lifetime. He recognized that it was not a once-and-done exchange, but an ongoing process: "The beginning of wisdom is this: Get wisdom. Though it cost all you have, get understanding" (Prov. 4:7). In other words, we take the first step in becoming sage by recognizing how essential wisdom is to us. As we do, our hearts, souls, minds, and strength are reoriented so we are growing toward teleios. Jesus' followers are called individually and corporately to participate in lifelong discipleship. This process is what becoming sage is all about.

For more than a decade, I've written and spoken about spiritual formation at midlife and beyond. As a result, I've heard a similar, sad refrain from hundreds of people all over the country: a high percentage of our churches tend to approach the task of discipleship with a strong focus on early-stage faith training. We pour lots of energy and money into ministry focused on children and families. And many congregations are deeply committed to equipping new believers with the basics of the faith. This is beautiful and important work.

The lack of emphasis on ongoing disciple-making among those further along in their journey with Jesus leads many to assume that simply repeating the same patterns they learned as new believers will sustain them throughout their days. While the practice of classic spiritual disciplines are foundational to spiritual growth, it is equally true that the questions, transitions, and shifts that take place at midlife and beyond call for different kinds of conversation, prayer, reflection, and response to God in order to cultivate teleios in our lives.

The most recent US census tells us that about a third of the population in this country is in the second half of their lives and is the fastest growing demographic in the country.[3] Other studies report that older adults are leaving or downshifting church involvement at a level comparable with that of millennials (those born between 1981 and 1996) and older members of Gen Z (those born after 1996).[4] There are many factors contributing to this quiet exodus among those in the second half of their lives, but the one I've heard repeatedly from many leavers (as well as those who are staying, but struggling) is that they feel they've "aged out" of their congregations, even though they haven't outgrown their faith.

The book you're holding in your hands offers individual readers, groups, and church leaders meaningful ways in which to cultivate fresh growth and ongoing fruitfulness for those of us growing through the latter seasons of our lives.

The first section of the book addresses the question, "What does it mean to become sage?" It explores ways in which we can better define and understand maturity.

The second section focuses on spiritual growth themes specific to those at midlife and beyond. Each chapter offers a thoughtful, biblically grounded discussion of topics relevant to those at midlife and beyond, including: church, family, friends, finances, our bodies, mental health, vocation, and the search for meaning.

Each chapter also includes questions for both individual reflection and group discussion designed to encourage readers to think through each of these themes in their own contexts.

We become sage as we recognize, then explore, how God is at work in the changes we're experiencing.

By the time we arrive at midlife, few of us believe there are one-size-fits-all formulas and pre-packaged curriculum that will decode the challenges we're facing. This book is designed to identify and begin to clarify the unique gifts and challenges of midlife discipleship, recognizing that there are no easy answers. You'll find companionship, information, and conversation meant to provoke growth, hope, and renewal in your life.

We become sage as we recognize, then explore, how God is at work in the changes we're experiencing. We become sage as we respond to Him with prayerful reflection, honest questions, thoughtful discussion, and possible recalibration of some of our life choices.

If we in the church are called to be a countercultural community, expanding our discipleship focus to include and embrace every life stage just might be one of the most countercultural things we can do in our youth-obsessed society. God doesn't offer us a fountain of youth. He is instead calling us toward maturity while promising fruitfulness in every season of our lives: "The righteous will flourish like a palm tree, they will grow like a cedar of Lebanon; planted in the house of the LORD, they will flourish in the courts of our God. They will still bear fruit in old age, they will stay fresh and green, proclaiming, 'The LORD is upright; he is my Rock, and there is no wickedness in him'" (Ps. 92:12–15).

This is the fruit that grows from a life that is becoming sage.

What does it mean to become sage?

CHAPTER 1

GROW UP!

Maturity Defined

I flunked my spiritual maturity test.

No, not the one that involves my everyday life. This spiritual maturity test was an online assessment[1] that promised to boil down my current faith practices and attitudes toward God into a tidy numerical score. I was asked to report honestly about my measurable behaviors, including how often I read my Bible, attended church, and gave away part of my income to God's work. I also had to quantify whether I had clarity on my purpose and goals, as well as how frequently I sensed God's presence in my daily life.

Taking a multiple-choice test was a modern American approach to measuring spiritual growth. The site offering the test suggested it be used as a way to quantify my current spiritual life and motivate me to make changes that might improve my score in the future. My final grade was a sobering 67 percent—a solid D. Does God grade on a curve?

Of course not. And while I understand that the survey developers intended to create a snapshot of a test taker's spiritual life, God doesn't use a yardstick to trace our growth. He employs something far more multifaceted: Are we growing in Christlikeness? Do we look more like Jesus today than we did yesterday?

Spiritual growth is not as simple as 1, 2, 3 . . . 67 percent. By the time we arrive at midlife, we know that the journey to maturity is as complex as our lives are.

A Barna Group survey of more than 1,000 adults found that there was great confusion around the subject of spiritual maturity. Researchers noted that though our culture has plenty of spiritual growth resources available, including churches, schools, camps, conferences, and a vast array of media options, there is a poverty when it comes to understanding what maturity looks like:

> Many churchgoers and clergy struggle to articulate a basic understanding of spiritual maturity. People aspire to be spiritually mature, but they do not know what it means. Pastors want to guide others on the path to spiritual wholeness, but they are often not clearly defining the goals or the outcomes of that process.[2]

The Barna survey revealed that we in the church have wildly differing ideas of what it means to become sage. When asked to define spiritual maturity, 20 percent of self-identified Christians couldn't answer the question at all. The other 80 percent offered responses that included having a relationship with Christ, following rules, choosing a moral lifestyle, practicing personal spiritual disciplines, possessing faith, applying the Bible's principles, and being involved in their local congregation.

Despite not being able to agree on what maturity is, more than half the adults surveyed reported that they believed they were spiritually healthy. In analyzing the results of the study, Barna Group president David Kinnaman said,

> As people begin to realize that the concepts and practices of spiritual maturity have been underdeveloped, the Christian community is likely to enter a time of renewed emphasis on discipleship, soul care, the tensions of truth and grace, the so-called "fruits" of the spiritual life, and the practices of spiritual disciplines.[3]

There have been some corporate-style efforts to help churches quantify spiritual growth in the years since Kinnaman made that hopeful prediction. For example, a church management software company suggests leaders who want to see spiritual growth happen in their local churches keep tabs on congregational involvement in weekly worship, small groups, serving, giving, and personal prayer and Bible study, then set measurable goals in order to increase those numbers.[4] The assumption built into a program like this is similar to the personal maturity survey I took online. If a person commits to weekly church attendance, involvement in a small group, personal devotional time, volunteering in a church ministry, and tithing faithfully, they must be moving toward maturity.

If you've been a follower of Jesus for more than twenty minutes, you probably realize that being active in the church doesn't automatically correlate to spiritual growth. Certainly, it can. But it can also mean that a church attender's calendar is simply full of Christian-y activities. Evangelist Billy Sunday once famously said, "Going to church doesn't make you a Christian any more than going to a garage makes you an automobile.[5]

HEY, YOU! HEARANDOBEY!

While believers are encouraged to obey Jesus' command to go into all the world and make disciples, per Matthew 28:18–20, it's been my experience that many translate His words to mean something like, "Probably you should consider becoming a cross-cultural missionary. If that doesn't work, then at least tell your coworkers you believe in Jesus and maybe invite them to a church event. If they receive Christ, encourage them to get baptized. Amen."

However, Jesus was speaking of something more fully encompassing than inviting a not-yet-believer to a church service, as valuable as that may be. He was telling His friends that their mission was to call others to turn to God via repentance evidenced in baptism, and then pattern both for and with them how to follow Jesus in the trenches of everyday life. This "go and show" command is infused with the promise of His presence every step of the journey from Jerusalem into the world He came to redeem.

Jesus didn't innovate this sort of whole-life, learn-as-you-go style of learning. He'd been raised in the household of people who lived the *Shema*, the ancient, core Hebrew prayer found in Deuteronomy 6:4–9. Shema means "Listen!", which carries the connotation of "Hey, you! Yes, you! Hearandobey!"—as if "hear" and "obey" were a single, unbroken word. *The Message* paraphrase of this passage captures the immersive nature of this calling:

> Attention, Israel!
> GOD, our God! GOD the one and only!
> Love GOD, your God, with your whole heart: love him with all that's in you, love him with all you've got!
> Write these commandments that I've given you today on your hearts. Get them inside of you and then get them inside your children. Talk about them wherever you are, sitting at home or walking in the street; talk about them from the time you get up in the morning to when you fall into bed at night. Tie them on your hands and foreheads as a reminder; inscribe them on the doorposts of your homes and on your city gates. (Deut. 6:4–9)

When the resurrected Jesus told His Jewish followers to go into the world and make disciples, He was not reinventing the proverbial wheel but applying to Himself the pattern each one had known, prayed, and lived from childhood. What was new was His promise of empowerment. This promise meant they'd be free to live out His command to love God fully, heart, soul, mind, and strength, and then express this love for Him by loving their neighbors in the same way they'd been loved into His life (Luke 10:27).

Loving God and neighbor is what everyday discipleship looks like. The late Dallas Willard noted that the word "apprenticeship" better captures what discipleship is for us moderns. He explained, "In the New Testament, discipleship means being an apprentice of Jesus in our daily existence. A disciple is simply someone who has decided to be with another person, under appropriate conditions, in order to learn to do what that person does, or to become what that person is."[6]

Apprenticing Jesus means seeking to remain in His company, learning from Him, and doing what we see Him doing. It enfolds every area of our lives, from cleaning the toilets and washing sheets after your six-year-old has the stomach flu to singing praises to Him during a worship service.

HEART, SOUL, MIND, STRENGTH

We moderns have developed some popular models of discipleship that are apprenticeship-lite in their emphasis. They tend to focus on one area of our lives to the neglect of other, equally important parts. See if any of these forms of discipleship resonate with your own apprenticeship experience:

The Insider's Club Disciple

When Paul encouraged his friends at Corinth to imitate him as he imitated the Messiah (1 Cor. 11:1), he was referencing the apprenticeship model he'd experienced in his own life, first as a Jewish boy, next as a disciple of Rabbi Gamaliel (Acts 22:3), and finally as a follower of Jesus. But in some churches, discipleship may be little more than Christian peer pressure. For example, if most of the women in your church homeschool their children and you work outside the home and send your children to public school, at an Insider's Club congregation, you'll feel the spoken and unspoken pressure to quit your job and begin homeschooling too. We see the pressure to conform to the group in churches where nonessentials like political affiliation become key to our identity among our brothers and sisters.

We all want to belong. Fear of being excluded or being branded as a problem or troublemaker trains us to perform our faith for an audience composed of imaginary Olympic judges, living for the elusive approval of the in-group. Their approval then becomes the measure for our maturity. Our heart's need to belong leads the way in this form of discipleship.

The Best Life Disciple

You may change the channel when you see a TV preacher promising health and wealth if only you have enough faith (and drop him or her a check in the mail). But because prosperity teaching tends to mirror the "pull yourself up by the bootstraps and you can succeed" language of the American Dream, we find more subtle versions of it lurking in some churches. When we hear that if we just apply these four (or six, or ninety-three) pithy biblical principles and our finances, marriage, or family will magically improve, we are hearing a watered-down version of prosperity preaching. When an attractive Christian leader's lifestyle and appearance are curated for sharing on social media, it is a way to sell the promise of a religious version of our culture's version of success. The goal of this form of discipleship is the blessing of the best life.

Though discussions of spiritual maturity usually aren't front and center in this model, benchmarks of the Best Life model have to do with a Christian-subculture approved, upwardly mobile, Instagrammable lifestyle. Fear of missing out drives Best Life behavior, but underneath that image-management lies a deeper, soul-level concern: If "they" knew the real you, would they love you? Does God?

The Bible Master Disciple

This form of discipleship is based on acquisition and demonstration of Bible knowledge. Loving God looks like citing Bible verses, listening to and quoting sermons, being able to use Scripture reference tools, attending seminary, reading books, and winning apologetics-type debates against anyone who does not hold to the same doctrinal positions as the Bible Master and his or her favorite theological or denominational team.

None of these things are wrong in and of themselves (after all, you're holding a book in your hands right now!), but a lopsided emphasis on knowledge acquisition means maturity will be defined primarily by intellectual aptitude when it comes to spiritual things. Those whose minds may not work in a way like this will always be treated as second-class Christians in Bible Master circles.

The Hamster Wheel Disciple

"Kathy is such a servant! She runs the nursery, organizes meals for those who are sick, folds and stuffs the bulletin every week, and runs the weekly prayer meeting." Communities committed to the Hamster Wheel model of discipleship celebrate service and more service, usually at and for the church: "Jim is a spiritual giant in our church. He's a deacon, in charge of the landscaping crew, leads the middle school youth group, and seems to be here every time the doors open."

Some who run marathons of church-service-on-a-hamster-wheel may not recognize that their need to be needed is not always the same thing as serving God. In Hamster Wheel congregations, maturity is measured in church-based volunteer hours. This form of discipleship is focused on strength, often to the diminishment of a person's heart, soul, and mind.

A person discipled under one of these systems may be malformed in their spiritual development, similar in form to someone who goes to the gym and does only bicep curls for a solid year. They'll end up with a lopsided physique—though they may be of great help carrying heavy packages up a couple of flights of stairs.

Decades ago, I witnessed the way an unbalanced version of discipleship shaped a church culture and eventually caused it to implode. The pastor, whose discipleship fell into the Bible Master category mentioned above, held advanced seminary degrees, but sadly, his relational and leadership abilities hadn't developed along with his brilliant mind. He often used his sermons to suppress anyone who disagreed with him and rarely apologized when his anger exploded in meetings.

Although the severity of these issues wasn't detectable at first, it soon became clear there was a disconnect between what this man knew about the Bible and the kind of character he possessed. Though for a while a steady stream of new people came to the church drawn by the preaching, the congregation never seemed to grow in size because others who'd been injured chose to leave. Eventually, the pace of leavers overtook the new arrivals, and the church dissolved under the unbalanced weight of lopsided leadership.

TOWARD MATURITY

Scripture uses the language of moving from infancy to adulthood in order to coach us toward maturity.[7] We will not grow in a healthy way by focusing on one area of our lives, such as the mind, while deemphasizing others, such as the soul, emotions, and body. Author J. Oswald Sanders describes the effects of lopsided growth:

> The spiritually immature person meets adult situations and tests with childish and immature reactions. This always produces tension and strain with all the attendant problems. When sorrow strikes, he is inclined to indulge in an orgy of self-centered emotion. If financial reverses come, he is at a loss to know why this should come to him, and he blames God. When hopes are dashed, he loses heart and drops his bundle. When adversity overtakes him, he is swallowed up in self-pity. In domestic difficulties he indulges in tantrums or sulks and creates an atmosphere that mars home unity. When placed with other difficult people, he falls prey to censorious criticism and "gives as good as he gets." When his will is thwarted by God or man, he becomes rebellious and bitter.[8]

Maturity isn't a fixed destination but describes a process of growth in Christlikeness in every area of life, through every season of life.

Maturity isn't a fixed destination but describes a process of growth in Christlikeness in every area of life, through every season of life. It is marked by an ongoing increase in self-giving love modeled in the ministry of Jesus and empowered by the Holy Spirit.[9] It is a generative, generous existence marked by ongoing ripening of the fruit of the Spirit and a steady increase in godly wisdom.[10] By definition, this kind of wisdom saturates our hearts, souls, minds, and strength.

Our foolish mistakes, detours, and sins as we grow can be transformed into wisdom as we submit ourselves to God. His goal for us is to be re-formed into the image of His beloved Son (2 Cor. 3:18). It is a far more comprehensive desire for our lives than becoming a member of an Insider's Club, living some version of a Best Life, winning at the Bible Master game, or running on a Hamster Wheel that goes nowhere.

Many of us don't discover how lopsided we are in our formation until we approach or enter midlife. The next chapter will discuss why that is. The good news about midlife is that God is at work for our good and His glory. No one wants us to become sage more than He does.

Midlife should unsettle us. My 67 percent score on that spiritual maturity test doesn't begin to measure the way He's been at work bringing me to completion. Some elements of that process, such as the practice of foundational spiritual disciplines like Bible reading, prayer, worship, and service/outreach don't change, no matter what our age.

But midlife also carries new gifts and challenges unique to this life stage, and our apprenticeship practices must reflect that. Why and how? Those questions will guide us as we explore them together in the pages of this book.

FOR INDIVIDUAL REFLECTION

1. In what ways have you seen growth toward maturity in your life? This question may contain the temptation for you to begin by listing all the ways you see yourself falling short or not measuring up. Try to fight that temptation. Instead, in the company of your Master, reflect on the positive ways He has been at work to move you toward loving Him heart, soul, mind, and strength over time.

2. As you've listed the positive areas of growth, do you notice a lopsided emphasis in one area of your life over another? If so, why might that be the case?

3. Take some time to prayerfully reflect on Philippians 3:12–15, with special consideration of the fact that the apostle Paul wrote this letter when he was well into midlife. How would you put this passage into your own words in order to coach someone else on their spiritual journey? What might the Holy Spirit be saying to you through Paul's words right now?

FOR GROUP CONVERSATION

1. Reflect on which model(s) of apprenticeship may be operating in your congregation: Insider's Club, Best Life, Bible Master, or Hamster Wheel. Or is there another version? If so, describe it.

2. Are heart, soul, mind, and strength nurtured in your community in a balanced, holistic way? If not, which elements seem to be emphasized most strongly? Why might that be?

3. Who do you know that seems to reflect spiritual maturity? Why do you say so? What stands out most to you about this person's experience and character?

Loving God heart, soul, mind, and strength is not separated into four different-but-related silos of our lives. Each is meant to be integrated so our one-and-only life is lived in growing communion with God. Becoming sage means becoming whole.

CHAPTER 2

MIDLIFE AND BEYOND

Deconstructing Life 1.0

When I had my first child, I pored over child development literature in search of information. What was the average age at which my baby would roll from back to tummy? When might she speak her first word? Take her first steps?

Parents become well-acquainted with the milestones of infant and child development via experience. We supplement that information with conversations with other parents ("Does your toddler have tantrums in the cereal aisle too?"), asking questions of our pediatrician, and reading books and websites.

Many of us are familiar with the first stages of development: infancy, toddlerhood, childhood, adolescence, and the transition to young adulthood. At that point, it may be easy to default to the idea that maybe adulthood is a little like a long, unbroken stretch of highway. We get on the entrance ramp and keep driving until we reach the end of the road.

However, adulthood has distinctive movements, each with different developmental tasks. In young adulthood, we're building our lives, making decisions about relationships, careers, and lifestyle. At midlife, we face shifts as seismic as they were during puberty as our bodies change, our nests empty, and our first-half-of-life ambitions tend to focus on making meaning of what's come before. And old age carries with it an entirely new set of challenges as both loss and the desire to leave a legacy shape our final days.

We recognize the path through adulthood is anything but a smooth stretch of highway. That road shifts with unexpected blind corners and zig-zagged switchbacks. The pavement may change from asphalt to cobblestones to quicksand.

I appreciated this observation from Father Richard Rohr:

> We are a "first-half-of-life culture," largely concerned about surviving successfully. Probably most cultures and individuals across history have been situated in the first half of their own development up to now, because it is all they had time for. . . . Our institutions and our expectations, including our churches, are almost entirely configured to encourage, support, reward, and validate the tasks of the first half of life.[1]

There's historical precedent for this: the average life expectancy in the US for a child born in 1900 was 47 years for white men, 49 years for white women, and 33 and 34 years for black men and women, respectively. Life expectancy for a child born in 2000 for all of these groups has increased to 75 years for white men, 80 years for white women, 68 years for black men, and 75 years for black women.[2]

In other words, fewer people were living into the second half of their lives until after World War II. During those postwar years, the rise in life expectancy for older adults living at the far end of the life spectrum was met and eclipsed by the Baby Boom. The massive numbers of boomers born into a relatively prosperous society led both popular culture and the church to focus on youth. Marketers aimed at the tastes and desires of the young. Influencers told us during the 1960s not to trust anyone over age thirty. We sang rock anthems about hoping to die before we got old.[3]

Frequently, the church followed suit. Worship music drew on the motifs and melodies embraced by youth of pop, folk, soul, and rock. Worship services used the liturgy of entertainment to draw spiritual seekers into the building. The youth-oriented Jesus Movement of the late 1960s and early 1970s ignited numerical growth of evangelical congregations for years afterward. But as time marched forward, some leaders began to notice that numbers didn't translate into spiritual depth.

Interestingly, one of first to address this dilemma was a then-influential, youth-oriented church that had been laser-focused on boomer seekers since its birth in the late 1970s. In 2005, megachurch Willow Creek Community Church in suburban Chicago commissioned a study about how its members and affiliates in other locations were growing in Christ. The *Reveal* study highlighted the fact that the more a person grew in their faith, the less they fit into the life of the church.[4] Those who were classified as being more mature spiritually using the metrics of the survey reported that they felt spiritually stuck at church and/or "stalled" in their faith journey.

The study made a big splash among church leaders when it was released, and many other congregations participated in follow-up surveys so they could take the temperature of their own churches. I've had a unique vantage point as I've worked at one seminary, been a student at another, blogged and written about this topic for many years, worked with many pastors in my area when I was a part of a church networking ministry, and have had the opportunity to visit a wide variety of evangelical churches with my husband in the years since *Reveal* first rolled out. Sadly, I didn't see much evidence that the study changed the way most churches approached spiritual formation for their maturing members.

WHAT DOES THE JOURNEY TO MATURITY LOOK LIKE?

There are parallels between human growth and development at every life stage and spiritual development as we continue to mature in our faith. Our faith *should* change as we grow: "When I was a child, I talked like a child, I thought like a child, I reasoned like a child. When I became a man, I put the ways of childhood behind me. For now we see only a reflection as in a mirror; then we shall see face to face. Now I know in part; then I shall know fully, even as I am fully known" (1 Cor. 13:11–12).

The pattern of human growth has much to reveal to us about what an always-maturing faith looks like. I am deeply grateful for the work of James Fowler[5] and Janet Hagberg and Robert Guelich,[6] who helped give language to the lifelong arc of spiritual growth. Their pioneering writing a generation ago highlighted the reality that just as we develop physically and emotionally in distinctive stages from infancy through old age, so healthy spiritual/moral development can be described in a similar manner. These writers identified that each stage of a growing spiritual life—from the infancy of first belief until the final, self-giving love of a matured faith—carries its own tasks and challenges. Fowler and the writing team of Hagberg and Guelich, as well as the many others who've built on their work, note that chronological age does not automatically translate into spiritual maturity. Some older believers may be stuck in a childish kind of faith; some younger believers grow deep roots more rapidly.

These writers identified six main stages that occur in an apprentice's journey of faith. I've found in each one a way to describe the soul's cry to know God and have discovered in the life of King David a helpful way in which to express and flesh out those concepts:

Stage 1: "God, I believe in You"

Some Stage 1 believers grow up in a Christian home and can't remember a time when they didn't know about God. Others may have grown up in a home where a faith different than Christianity was practiced, or in a family with no religious affiliation at all. Whether it is in infancy or at a later point in life, we begin our journey with an awareness or awakening to the reality of the God of the Bible.

If we've been born into a home where faith is practiced, this growing awareness may mirror our passage through childhood. If we come to faith in Jesus during our teens or adulthood, we may begin our journey with Him by praying a prayer or making a commitment that changes our status from "lost" to "found." No matter what our age, the first stage of our faith walk is often marked with a sense of simplicity and child-like wonder in our new relationship with God. That simplicity may translate into a reliance on slogans and formulas as we take our first steps with Him.

We can see what Stage 1 faith looks like as we glance at David's family history. His great-grandmother and great-grandfather's remarkable betrothal story is captured in the book of Ruth; he was born into a God-fearing family. In 1 Samuel 16:1–13, the prophet Samuel invited David's father, Jesse, to worship with him before prayerfully assessing each of Jesse's sons as he sought to anoint a king who would replace the spiritually compromised Saul. Youngest son David wasn't even in the house at the time. He was tending the family's sheep. But when they brought this young man before Samuel, God made it clear that David was the one He'd been looking for because David was "a man after his own heart" (1 Sam. 13:14).

We see evidence of David's "God, I believe in You" faith not only through his willing submission to the unexpected calling on his life, but in the reputation he'd gotten as a lyre-playing song-crafter who'd been worshiping God in the hills outside the family home in Bethlehem as he was tending sheep. Sweetness and trust characterized David's young faith.

After his encounter with Samuel, David is called from the sheep herd into the service of King Saul. Saul's rebellion against God opened the door to spiritual torment. For a time, the musical praise that emerged from David's childhood faith brought Saul respite from the evil that howled in Saul's soul (1 Sam. 16:14–23).

Stage 2: *"God, I belong to You"*

Young faith seeks structure, and as we continue to grow, young believers find this structure by becoming a part of a church or fellowship group. Stage 2 faith is all about learning the written (and unwritten) rules of how we live our faith within community. There's a sense of security and excitement as we discover our spiritual identity in the context of a group and form friendships with other believers just like us. In order to belong, we may try to play down experiences and ideas that don't align with the group's style or congregation's doctrine.

We can see notes of this stage in David's spiritual development as a young adult, as well as his movement toward leadership and Stage 3 faith. When the chosen people found themselves at war with the Philistines, David's older siblings joined Saul's army, but David recognized that his role as a youngest son in his family and community was to stay behind and care for his father's flocks. After the sons failed to return home after a forty-day standoff with the Philistines and their supersized leader, Goliath, David's father sent him with some provisions for his older sons and the commander of the unit.

When David arrived, he spoke as a fully committed member of his community: "What will be done for the man who kills this Philistine and removes this disgrace from Israel? Who is this uncircumcised Philistine that he should defy the armies of the living God?" (1 Sam. 17:26). His older brothers mocked his zeal, but Saul saw the holy fire in David's soul and attempted to garb him in his own armor. Young David felt awkward and constricted in the heavy gear, expressing a bit of independence in the pressured situation. He instead resorted to the weapons he knew best from his sheepherding experience: stones and a sling. He met the giant Philistine on the battlefield, proclaiming his trust ". . . in the name of the LORD Almighty, the God of the armies of Israel, whom you have defied" (1 Sam. 17:45). David found his identity in his God and among his people. But he didn't stop there.

Stage 3: "God, I'm working for You"

The next stage of spiritual growth is focused on doing things *for* God. This often expresses itself in the form of taking on greater areas of service or responsibility within your church. Authors Janet Hagberg and Robert Guelich note that Stage 3 faith tends to brim with activity: "It is positive and dynamic, centered on being productive in the area of our faith. It nourishes us because it is so personally rewarding, even when the objective is to help others. In helping or leading, we also are fed, so it operates on goals and achievements, building and creating."[7]

You might find yourself at this stage teaching Sunday school or volunteering at a food pantry, working for God. David found himself at this point of his apprenticeship fleeing a rage-filled enemy—King Saul. David was on the run from Saul for a long time.[8] This series of trials and tests trained his character while growing his commitment to God and his people. Even when David had two different opportunities to kill Saul, he chose not to do so out of respect for God and the office of king in his culture (1 Sam. 24, 26).

David had begun leading followers (1 Sam. 27:2) who were attracted to his nimble, creative, faithful-to-God style of leadership. When Saul was killed by the hand of an enemy, David was ready to step into the role for which he'd been anointed as a younger man (2 Sam. 2) even as he continued to fight soldiers still loyal to Saul. Though he'd been tested from without, the real test of David's character would come from within once he'd arrived at the pinnacle of his Stage 3 service to God.

Stage 4: "God, where are you? I'm alone in the dark"

If we're continuing to grow, we will most likely at some point move from an earlier sense of abundance and fellowship to what St. John of the Cross famously described as "the dark night of the soul." This dark night is an existential sense of loss or disorientation. It may accompany a loss or transition, such as the death of a family member or close friend, children leaving home, or a workplace layoff, but is not always connected to an inciting incident. It can also grow from the question, "Is this all there is?"

This dark night . . . may accompany a loss or transition. It can also grow from the question "Is this all there is?"

As we enter Stage 4, we may find that the youthful innocence, group identity, and baptized ambition that supported our growth to this point is being pruned away. However, that pruning often feels like amputation as we must reassess who we are and what we believe about God and the world around us. Author Madeleine L'Engle's thoughts on the middle years being the "decisive period in our lives" speak more to personal maturity than to the stages of faith; however, her words also ring true for the

Stage 4 experience: "All the protective covering of the first three stages [childhood, adolescence, early adulthood] is gone, and we are suddenly alone with ourselves and have to look directly at the great and unique problem of the meaning of our own particular existence in this particular universe."[9]

Authors Hagberg and Guelich call this dark night period "the Wall" and explain that the key task of this stage is to learn to surrender to God in more mature ways. They note, "Not everyone goes through the Wall. Some stop or get stuck at earlier stages in the journey and never get to the Wall. Others decide at the Wall to return to an earlier stage. Still others get stuck in front of the Wall, not wanting to submit to God."[10]

There are no shortcuts through this difficult stage, which often presents itself at midlife in the form of losses and transitions. If we navigate Stage 4 well, we'll discover we're growing from certainty toward humility as we learn to walk with God through our darkness. Our darkness is not dark to Him (Ps. 139:12).

David found himself at Stage 4 after he'd become king and vanquished his enemies. Israel enjoyed a period of unprecedented wholeness and peace. This should have been the pinnacle of David's experience, but from that height, David took a deep moral fall as he used his position to force himself on another man's wife, then schemed to have that man killed in the line of battle. David then took the woman he impregnated, Bathsheba, to become another one of his wives. How could a man who'd once been so courageous and faithful have taken such a dramatic fall into sin?

It seems that the same wiles David used when he was on the run from Saul were no longer a strength, but a temptation.

What worked for him in Stages 1, 2, and 3 became a snare for him in Stage 4. God sent the prophet Nathan to unmask David's scheming and sin. In humility, David owned his sin and accepted the consequence of his actions (Ps. 51). The child he had with Bathsheba would die, along with David's pride.

When the baby was born and became ill, David prostrated himself before God, fasting and pleading for mercy for the little one. The child died a week later. David's terrified servants were frantic about the possibility he'd break down when they delivered the agonizing news (2 Sam. 11–12:23). To their surprise, he rose from his anticipatory grief, now chastised, humbled, and submissive to God. He was a more spiritually mature man.

A few years later, David faced more loss when his son Absalom murdered his half brother, Ammon, who'd raped Absalom's sister Tamar (2 Sam. 13:14). Absalom was eventually killed, and you can hear David's torn heart in the words he cried upon learning the news: "O my son Absalom! My son, my son Absalom! If only I had died instead of you—O Absalom, my son, my son!" (2 Sam. 18:33). Grief mellowed David, and as he moved through the darkness of this period in his life, he emerged an increasingly sage man.

Stage 5: "God, I'm ready to pass along what You've given me"

If we persevere through the darkness, eventually we will find ourselves on the other side of it. Our faith will not look like a bigger, better version of Stages 2 or 3. We will no longer be motivated by ambition to do Big Things for God. Stage 5 faith is focused on discovering the richness of living in companionship *with* God. It is in this stage of growth that we move toward generativity, where the focus of our activity comes in passing along the wisdom born of our life experience and our communion with God. It is exceedingly rare to arrive at this place in our younger years. It takes the process of building through Stages 1, 2, and 3 and then the dismantling of Stage 4 to move us into this period of growth.

As the darkness began to lift in King David's life, we find him preparing Solomon, the child born to him and Bathsheba after their first child died, to ascend to the throne. The effects of this preparation are most evident when we consider what Solomon asked of God at the beginning of his own reign over Israel. He didn't request power or a larger kingdom. Instead, he asked God for wisdom, which was a value passed on to him from his father (1 Kings 3:7–9).

One of the consequences of David's sin earlier in his life occurred when God told him he would not be permitted to build a temple in Jerusalem for God to replace the mobile tabernacle that had centered the worship of His people to that point (1 Chronicles 17). This provided David ample motivation to pass on what he knew of God to his son Solomon.

Quite possibly, Psalm 131 was written during this period of David's life. The words of this psalm capture the tenderness, intimacy, and desire to pass on his faith that is characteristic of Stage 5:

> My heart is not proud, LORD,
>   my eyes are not haughty;
> I do not concern myself with great matters
>   or things too wonderful for me.

But I have calmed and quieted myself,
  I am like a weaned child with its mother;
  like a weaned child I am content.

Israel, put your hope in the LORD
  both now and forevermore.

Stage 6: *"God, I'm coming home"*

A faith moving toward completion is marked by an ever-deepening surrender to God as life on earth is relinquished to Him and we prepare for death. This quiet, reflective period may be marked by physical suffering and will certainly be marked with the accumulated grief of losses of family and friends. But this time will also be a spiritually rich period that welcomes and integrates the growth of all the earlier periods. Stage 6 is marked by God's love and compassion for others and self.

An older friend told me she realized a shift had happened in her life when she noticed that the youthful optimism she once possessed about life didn't apply in the same way as she aged. "Things are not going to get 'better' in the ways I once expected they would. I am moving toward the end." She was not without hope. But her statement highlighted for me that she was preparing to say goodbye to this life and be with the Lord she'd loved since childhood.

Young David began his life with God as a child playing the lyre and singing to Him. David's Stage 6 final recorded words were a song to God too. In 2 Samuel 23, David praised God for the guidance of the Spirit of the Lord to and through him, remembered the everlasting covenant He'd made with David's descendants,[11] and urged his beloved people to flee from evil. Childlike (not childish) trust flowered in his life. He was ready to go home to meet God face to face.

GROWING UP AGAIN

It's important to remember that growth doesn't always follow a tidy trajectory. Just as an eleven-year-old may one day seem to be a teenager and then the next day a kid again, so it is with a living, growing faith.

The transitions of midlife can feel like a major challenge to that faith. In my early forties, my mother died, my husband and I relocated, and we went through an excruciating upheaval at a church where I served on staff. If that wasn't enough, our kids were leaving the nest, and I was in perimenopause, experiencing the hormonal swings of adolescence seemingly set in reverse. We were dealing with the mental illness of a relative. My husband faced job uncertainty. A couple of key friendships in my life were changing. Darkness surrounded me and welled up within me.

With 20/20 hindsight, I now realize I believed that the strength of my Stage 3 faith would vault me effortlessly through those challenges. I'd been a gung-ho church volunteer and was involved in many other ministry initiatives over the years too. In the darkness of my midlife experience, I longed for the relative simplicity of an earlier version of my faith and life. Or perhaps I hoped a new and improved version of that faith would blossom as a result of enduring these trials.

I discovered there are no shortcuts. I sought help and solace for my spiritual disorientation at church only to discover the focus on first-half-of-life issues such as marriage, parenting, or finances meant few were talking about spiritual formation in the second half of life.

Writer and videographer Steve Stockman observed:

> The evangelical wing of the Church spends a lot of energy on being "born again" but little time on "growing up" again. There is a failing to encourage newborn believers out of the maternity ward and into a big world where they will spend the rest of their spiritual lives trying to find what they are looking for.[12]

We can do better. What does it look like to grow up again as we move into our second adulthood? What is the nature of the apprenticeship journey as we face the challenges, changes, and blessings of middle age?

The next section of this book will offer a look at some key discipleship issues that work themselves out in new ways at midlife and beyond. Learning to discern the purposes and work of the Holy Spirit as we navigate these shifts and challenges will change the way in which both individuals and church communities approach the apprenticeship journey for and with those in the second half of our lives.

FOR INDIVIDUAL REFLECTION

1. As you read through the descriptions of the stages of faith development, what stands out to you most strongly? Why might that be the case?

2. Stage 4 seems to be a disruption in the upward trajectory of the previous three stages. Why do you think this is? Are you seeing that in your own life?

3. As you read through the words of Psalm 131, quoted at the end of the description of Stage 5, what questions arise for you at this moment in your life? Turn those questions into a prayer.

FOR GROUP CONVERSATION

1. In what ways do you most notice our culture's focus on youth/ the first half of life?

2. How do you see this "first half" focus working itself out in the church? In your own congregation?

3. The *Reveal* study pointed out that the more a person grew in their faith, the less they fit into the life of the church. Why do you think that might be? Is this a good thing or a bad thing? How do these findings fit with the information in this chapter about the stages of faith?

The process of becoming sage happens throughout every age and stage of development. Recognizing how growth and transformation happens can help us better surrender to changes we will experience over our own lifetime.

How can we cultivate spiritual maturity in the second half of life?

CHAPTER 3

GOING TO CHURCH, BEING THE CHURCH

*A sage's shifting relationship with their
local congregation*

Tracy* estimated she'd heard at least 2,350 sermons in her life-time. She'd been attending church since she was born, first with her parents, then as a gung-ho member of her youth group, then with her husband and their growing family. Now at age 45, Tracy had questions that didn't lend themselves to the kind of answers those Sunday morning sermons appeared to offer. Why did it seem that she remembered so little of what she heard over the years? Why hadn't her church attendance resulted in a noticeably transformed life? Why did she feel so disconnected from God?

When he was born again as a young adult, Steve* plunged into the life of his local church and eventually rose to a position of lay leadership in his nondenominational congregation. He felt he was using his gifts well as he served as an elder, led a small group, and helped out in the nursery. But eventually, he realized an incredible amount of his time was spent both in those elder meetings and in lots of other conversations surrounding the revelation that the church's youth pastor had sexually abused at least six high school students over the last decade. Though most in the congregation felt that the leadership team had handled the situation adequately, 47-year-old Steve felt as though the protracted behind-the-scenes struggles had drained his soul dry. How had so many missed the warning signs about this guy? Why had God allowed this terrible thing to happen to those young girls? Did the people at church really believe the words they spoke and sang and prayed about God? Did he?

"It's time for your meds." Karen* helped her mom into a sitting position, shifting the tired pillow behind her. Her mom's crooked half-smile in response surfaced an aching, familiar thought in Karen's heart: *What I wouldn't give to see my mom's old smile.* That smile was now a relic found in old photographs since a series of strokes had left the aging widow unable to care for herself. Karen flipped on the TV so the two of them could watch a Sunday morning church service together. It had been four years since her mom's stroke and four years since Karen had been able to attend church regularly. One old friend from the congregation where she'd been a member for years kept in touch via phone call or quick visit every so often, but no one else—friend or church leader—had ever reached out to her to find out how she was doing or if she needed anything since the "We'll pray for you" email at the time of her mom's initial medical crisis. *Out of sight, out of mind,* Karen thought sadly as she reached up to wipe some droplets of water that trickled from the drooping side of her mom's smile.

STATUS: IT'S COMPLICATED

Do you know someone like Tracy, Steve, or Karen? More than a decade ago, I began blogging occasionally about midlife-related themes. As a result, people began telling me their stories—and many of these stories had to do with their experiences at church. After hearing dozens of anecdotes over the years, I put together an informal, completely unscientific survey asking people over age 40 what their relationship was like with their local congregation.[1] As I wasn't a well-known blogger, I offered respondents entry into a drawing for a Starbucks gift card, hoping to net maybe fifty or even a hundred responses. The key questions on my survey were, "Are you more, less, or just as involved with your local church as you were ten years ago?" and "Why?"

I received more than five hundred responses, and most of them continued to pour in long after I'd awarded the gift card. I realized people were eager to share their stories. Here's a sampling of what they told me:

About half reported that midlife afforded them fresh opportunities for growth, ministry, and relationship.[2]

- "I am a former atheist who started attending church with my family. Ten years ago, I was not attending any church."
- "I want to reach the world for Christ through a mobilized local church."

- "Being a part of a local congregation is a way of life. Church is not about me."
- "I realize the importance of community, sharing gifts, and especially coming alongside the next generation."
- "I'm in leadership now."
- "More opportunity and time to serve."

The other half of those responding to the survey told me they'd downshifted or ended entirely their involvement with their local church.

- "It's hard to find a church that's not just a social club."
- "I'm not sure I see the point in most of what's being done there anymore."
- "I don't have the energy to deal with church politics. I'm burned out."
- "Very little sense of community and congregational care. The emphasis is on children and youth."
- "Fewer opportunities for service without going through a multi-year training program, and then being allowed only to teach the pre-defined lesson for the week."
- "When my life became turbulent, I was quickly branded a problem. No support."

There were some key themes that surfaced among the latter group. Challenges to meaningful connection in a congregation included caregiving and/or work responsibilities, church programming focused primarily on families with children or teens in the home, shifting or growing faith that was no longer in sync with the life of a congregation, and exhaustion with the drama of church politics.

Some of you reading this list may want to cry, "But Hebrews 10:24–25 says, 'And let us consider how we may spur one another on toward love and good deeds, not giving up meeting together, as some are in the habit of doing, but encouraging one another—and all the more as you see the Day approaching.' People should do all they can to go to church even if it doesn't meet their needs. They need to be there because God commands it and because their presence can make a difference for someone else."

I surmised that the seemingly negative comments from respondents didn't reflect selfishness, but rather the realities of midlife. Let's take a few moments to look at how those realities can change and reforge our involvement and connection at church before addressing the meaning of the imperative given us in Hebrews 10:24–25.

MAKING A LIVING, CAREGIVING

Caregiving or health issues sideline a fair percentage of formerly active church members. Some congregations have home visitation teams set up to provide ongoing connection with those who can no longer attend church regularly. But many caregivers or those with chronic health issues fall through the cracks.

I've experienced this. My husband and I became part-time caregivers for our grandchildren when they were young and their parents worked unpredictable hours. We were once children's ministry regulars at church, but our caregiving responsibilities meant we could no longer commit to that level of involvement or attendance. It was discouraging to realize that no one at church cared about why we'd stepped back from ministry. The only service that seemed to be valued were the things we did at the church, for the church.

Caregivers for the chronically ill also face the challenge of well-meaning church members not being able to sustain commitment to them for the long haul. One friend with a husband who'd been chronically ill for many years told me, "People have about a six-month window for active care of someone in a crisis. If the crisis becomes chronic, it can be difficult to find people in a church who will stick with you for the long haul, especially if you have an ongoing need for help."

Another pressure on the time of older members is career. Some find themselves at the pinnacle of their climb up the corporate ladder during these years. They're juggling heavy workplace responsibilities. Others have been downsized and are juggling multiple jobs in order to pay the bills. Author Amy Simpson observed that some congregational leaders may not always think through their expectations about the ways in which they call on their members to volunteer their non-work hours to the church:

> One youth pastor told me he expected my volunteer efforts to be like a part-time job. I didn't have time or energy for a part-time job on top of my full-time work. And if I had, I might have looked for one that paid. But I didn't want to "sit on the sidelines," so I exhausted myself to help in a ministry that needed people very different from me . . .

Because church ministry is their job and their passion, [church leaders] may not realize what it takes to give time and energy as a volunteer on top of jobs and family responsibilities. Because they're driven by exciting visions of all the church could do if they only had enough volunteer energy, they may lose sight of whether others are actually called and equipped to fulfill their visions. They may not understand that many people are exercising their spiritual gifts in ministries outside the church's walls. And they may not realize how difficult it is for people to say no to pastors.[3]

While many of us at midlife discover we have additional time, expertise, and gifts to offer at church, it can also be true that others in our ranks are using their gifts and giving of their time outside the church walls. It is right for a church leader to make a prayerfully considered ask of church members, challenging them to sacrificial service. And it is right, too, for the church to bless, honor, and provide care and support to those who are serving God in their workplace or by changing the diaper of a grandchild.

HEY, KIDS!

Some survey respondents noted that once children left the nest, they came to the realization that most of their church's programming was targeted at families with children under eighteen. A few people confessed to me over the years they didn't notice the family focus while their own families were benefitting from it.

I heard it in responses to my survey, such as, "The church is geared to young people, they don't need me or care about my opinion," and "I'm tired of the same programs year after year. I want deeper relationships with fewer people and more spiritual exercises like prayer and meditation than the canned studies offered at my congregation." Boomers fueled the growth in youth-focused church culture in the evangelical world. The same culture they helped create is now leaving some of them excluded as they move out of their active child-rearing years.

If we are becoming sage, we are also coming to terms with the fact that filling a slot on a church org chart may be a sign of a person's church commitment, but it is not a measure of their spiritual maturity.

Of course, once we've "aged out" of our church's family-centered programming, there are ways to continue to connect, serve, worship, and learn—and many of us do. We can serve as mentors (more about this in chapter 5). We can help create community by staying involved in Bible studies, small groups, or Sunday school classes. We can choose to step into lay leadership roles. But if we are becoming sage, we are also coming to terms with the fact that filling a slot on a church org chart may be a sign of a person's church commitment, but it is not a measure of their spiritual maturity.

Some survey respondents reminded me that there is another group that has long struggled to find a place in the local church—singles. My single friends have told me they often feel as though they're continually pushing their folding chairs up to a table that seems to be set only for couples and families. The US Census Bureau reported that in 2017, 45.2 percent of all Americans were single.[4] At midlife, many singles feel (even more acutely) the disconnect between family-centric church culture and their own experience.

Those who don't fit into the prevailing culture in our churches are perhaps the most meaningful measure of a congregation's spiritual health (Matt. 25:31–46). If there's no meaningful place in a church for singles—or those who are seen as less desirable in the eyes of our society (too old, too poor, too sick, too troubled, too weird)—then there's no safe place for anyone.

FAITH SHIFTS

I heard from many people who'd decreased their level of involvement at their present congregation, changed churches/denominations, or chose to stop attending church entirely because they felt they'd outgrown the church of their young adulthood.

I've met few church leaders who believe that anyone could "outgrow" their congregation. Think about it. When was the last time you heard a church leader explain in glowing terms the departure of a long-time member who's chosen a different faith community? "Ken and Julie have left our beloved Baptist church to join the Anglican congregation across town because they believe God has called them there, and frankly, we don't have much to offer them beyond great preaching (if I do say so myself!) and Ken's role as one of our building caretakers. We understand our church is better at developing young believers than it is at helping people finish their journey toward maturity at faith stages 4, 5, and 6. They'll be able to use their gifts of encouragement and service in new ways as they step into ministry at the church. We pray Ken and Julie find rich growth and deeper connection with God in their new congregation. We love them and thank God for the years we've shared together in this church."

Are Ken and Julie being selfish church consumers? Are they just moving on to greener pastures instead of sacrificially serving their current congregation? These are questions worth asking. The answer would require honesty in conversation with current church leaders and discernment in prayer as part of the leaving process. But part of that discernment process should include exploring whether they've outgrown their current church.

Others decide they're done with the institution of church altogether. Sociologists Josh Packard and Ashleigh Hope researched people who'd left the church but not their faith. Though Packard and Hope's study wasn't focused specifically on those at midlife, what they found mirrored some of what I was hearing in my informal survey too. The pair entered their study with the hypothesis that people had headed for the exit doors of their congregations because their faith had shifted or because they'd been wounded by the abuse, moral failing, or hypocrisy of a church leader. Certainly, there are many, many of those people, but the sociologists discovered that there was something just as powerful at work in the lives of many of the leavers they studied.

"As it turns out, none of these hypotheses was correct," Packard and Hope wrote. "Instead, it became clear to us that the story of the dechurched was the story of modern religious organizations and institutions stifling people's ability to engage with each other and their communities. . . . they flee the church not because they hate the church. They have in fact, worked tirelessly on behalf of the church. They flee for their own spiritual safety, to reconnect with a God they feel has been made distant to them by the structure of religion as practiced in organizations."[5]

There are plenty of questions church leaders may debate about what congregational membership means, and what, if any, connection they may have to people who've chosen to declare themselves "done" with church. But the number of those who feel they're outgrowing or leaving their churches is continuing to climb. It will take creativity and commitment for some congregations to find

At midlife, those who've been wounded by intramural battles at their local church begin to recalculate the cost.

ways to minister to and learn from both groups, who are beloved and essential members of the body of Christ.

BURNED OUT ON CHURCH POLITICS

If you've been a part of a church for any length of time, you've probably witnessed some power struggles in your congregation. Even healthy churches experience internal conflict over everything from ministry direction to carpet color. At midlife, those who've been wounded by intramural battles at their local church begin to recalculate the cost. In my informal survey, I heard heartbreaking statements like, "I was betrayed by my leaders again and again," "I'm tired of unresolved conflict," and "I am a survivor of spiritual abuse."

We are living in a time when some abusive or controlling

leaders are being exposed. It is a mark of God's love for us that the evil that has taken place in the darkness is being brought to light (Luke 8:17; 1 Cor. 4:5). But exposure also reveals the wounds of those who've been affected directly or indirectly by these events.

The cumulative effect of a couple of devastating experiences with toxic church leaders contributed to my own dark night of the soul at midlife. Professional counseling, support and accountability from friends, the passage of time, careful boundaries, and a commitment to forgive as I've been forgiven have helped me move forward. But it wasn't easy. Even now, there are times I struggle to trust those in a position of authority.

Almost every New Testament epistle was penned to address conflict or error within a local congregation. At midlife, as we're beginning to come to terms in deep, existential ways with the reality that our days on earth are limited, we may recognize what a drain of our emotional and spiritual resources many of these church conflicts have been. Those who've downshifted from active involvement in their local congregation because they're burned out on church politics are choosing health. It may take a long time before they're ready to engage at the level they once did. Or they may choose never again to commit in the same way. While those who are burned out face the real temptation to get bogged down in bitterness, true friends and good, gentle leaders have an opportunity to simply walk alongside those recovering from hurt and trauma.

DON'T GIVE UP MEETING TOGETHER . . . BUT

Those at midlife who've downshifted or ceased involvement in their local church because they've invested their energies outside the four walls of their church in service to God, those who've felt they've outgrown their church, those who feel they're done with church, and those who are burned out have likely heard someone quote Hebrews 10:24–25 as a way to encourage them to show up and be more involved at church.

The verses ("And let us consider how we may spur one another on toward love and good deeds, not giving up meeting together, as some are in the habit of doing, but encouraging one another—and all the more as you see the Day approaching") do indeed encourage gathering together. However, the passage is not about shaming people into attending a church service on Sunday mornings.

These verses emphasize everyday mutuality in our relationships as we urge one another in community toward lives characterized by love and good works, in light of the fact that the end of days grows ever nearer. One commentator noted, "The author is here saying . . . let us consider one another, taking into account and weighing our neighbor's circumstances and especially his risks, but this with a view not to exasperating criticism, but 'with a view . . . to incite them to love and good work,' acknowledging honest endeavor and making allowance for imperfection."[6]

In other words, this passage is a reminder that it is our job to pursue meaningful expressions of fellowship whenever we gather with other believers. We remember that commitment to a local body of believers is the primary way in which these relationships are formed, as well as the place in which we share together in corporate worship, learning, communion, and service. But we must also remember that Hebrews 10:24–25 isn't a goad to get us to attend church. It describes the nature of our lives together, whether we meet at church or run into another believer in the frozen food aisle at the grocery store.

FLOURISHING IN THE CHURCH

About half of those who responded to my survey said they were equally or more engaged in the life of their church as they'd been a decade earlier. This tells me that many of them were indeed experiencing a good measure of Hebrews 10:24–25 life together in their church communities. This goodness characterized this group's responses to my questions: "I'm less busy with my secular profession, which allows more time for church and mission/ministry-related activities," and "the hospitality, love and guidance at my church has helped me know God loves me and helps me worship and praise Him."

People growing toward spiritual maturity recognize that church isn't meant to be a destination, but a launch pad.

Generations of us have learned to talk about church as a destination. We go to church. We invite others to come to church with us. People growing toward spiritual maturity recognize that church isn't meant to be a destination, but a launch pad. Our gathering together as the people of God is meant to encourage, stretch, challenge, and nurture us with the goal of sending us into the world in mission. The congregational leaders who best understand this may be the ones who can do the work to begin exploring what that might look like for those in the second half of their lives.

FOR INDIVIDUAL REFLECTION

1. How would you describe your current relationship with your local church? Are you more, less, or just as involved as you were a decade ago? Why?

2. Meditate on Hebrews 10:24–25 in light of what it tells you about your life together with other believers, rather than using it as a rationale for measuring church attendance. What might the Holy Spirit be saying to you through these verses?

3. As you consider other Christians you may know who are your age or older, do you see them growing in their commitment and service to their local church? Or have they downshifted as a result of one of the following?

- Increased caregiving or workplace responsibilities
- A disconnect between focus on family ministry and their own life stage
- A faith shift
- Burnout due to church politics

Spend some time praying for each one by name, asking the Lord how you might encourage them in the coming days.

FOR GROUP CONVERSATION

1. Does your church function as a destination or a launch pad? Why do you say so?

2. How has your church community responded in the past to those who've quietly downshifted their involvement or drifted away entirely?

3. Make a list of midlife and older members at your church. (Include those who have become far less engaged or have disappeared from your midst during the last few years.) What might it look like in the context of your church community to reach out to this group to find out how to better support, bless, and resource them? Some possible examples based on the categories in this chapter include:

- Pray regularly and publicly for the deepening of the ministry of those already committed to your congregation.
- Pray regularly and publicly for those who are committed to caregiving or workplace duties. Reach out to caregivers regularly to find out what kind of support they may need from the congregation (visits, help with practical tasks such as small household repairs, rides to doctor visits, meals).
- Engage in frank self-evaluation about the focus of the church's ministry: Are you emphasizing reaching out and caring only for families with children under 18 to the exclusion of other demographic groups? Consider why this might be and what steps you might take to change this.
- Ask if you are willing to bless those who've left your church in search of a congregation that might be a better fit for them.
- Consider how the culture of your church may be burning out committed members.

Becoming sage means affirming that we in the body of Christ are not meant to grow alone. Our relationship with our local church may be changing, but that doesn't exempt us from the community-based disciplines of corporate prayer and worship, spiritual friendship, service, and learning. It does, however, call us to discern where and how God is calling us to serve Him at this stage of our lives.

CHAPTER 4

WE HEART FAMILY

*The gifts and challenges of changing
family relationships*

Imagine with me that you're a time traveler who is zapped from the present to a time shortly after Joseph and his family were reunited in Egypt after more than a decade[1] of separation (Gen. 46). You join the family as they sit over a lingering meal retelling their family history. They speak of Abram's family in Ur, recount with a sense of worshipful wonder Abraham's call from God, and describe the details of his journeys with Sarai and his nephew Lot. They remember their miracle forebear Isaac and their half uncle, Esau.

The patriarch of the gathering, Jacob, regales you all with stories of his youth. You're struck with the honesty with which the family talks about the stresses and rivalries that tore them apart. Their conversation is marked with a palpable sense of forgiveness and humility. Each one affirms with awe all the ways God has been at work in their imperfect family.

They ask you to tell them about what life is like in the future. After telling them a Savior for the whole world would be born from their line, you describe the new community, the church, that would be grafted into Israel's story.

"What does that new community look like?" Joseph asks you. The rest of the group falls silent, waiting to hear what you will say.

You try to summarize the exodus; the chosen people's journey back to the land of Israel; the Babylonian captivity; the journey of some of the chosen people back to the land of Israel; the birth, ministry, death, resurrection, and ascension of Jesus; and two thousand years of church history as succinctly as possible. Then you explain that the church in your day and time has many different expressions throughout the earth.

You tell them about the coarseness of modern culture and describe some of the ways this culture seems to devalue family. Then you list all the books, seminars, camps, and sermons designed to show God followers how to create a God-honoring marriage and family. You explain that couples expect to feel a sense of romantic love (after explaining what that is, as the notion was not common in the Ancient Near East), have happy, well-adjusted children, and shine as perfect exemplars of Jesus the Messiah in a dark and difficult world.

There's a long pause. You've given them a lot to consider. Then Benjamin speaks at last, "Sounds like maybe a perfect family might be a little like an idol for some of your people."

Joseph smiles as he looks around the room, "I don't think our family would measure up to your standards." The rest nod and laugh. He continues, "I cherish each one of you but could never make a god of a family like ours. After all, there's only one true God, blessed be His name."

WE ARE FAMILY

Playwright George Bernard Shaw said, "A happy family is but an earlier heaven."[2] Those words capture a glimmer of the goodness of life in the garden of Eden. Building a family was essential to the way in which Adam and Eve were to honor God's command to be fruitful and subdue the earth (Gen. 1:28). After the fall, Scripture continues to emphasize the way in which God uses family to pass on faith (Deut. 6:4–9) and provide care and shelter to its most vulnerable members (Ps. 68:6). There is a focus on the family in two of the Ten Commandments: the fifth commandment about honoring parents, and the seventh commandment prohibiting adultery, which sets a boundary around marriage.

Children are a gift from God (Ps. 127:3), yet Jesus calls us to love the Giver more than we love the gift:

> "Anyone who loves their father or mother more than me is not worthy of me; anyone who loves their son or daughter more than me is not worthy of me. Whoever does not take up their cross and follow me is not worthy of me. Whoever finds their life will lose it, and whoever loses their life for my sake will find it." (Matt. 10:37–39)

We hold those words in tension with the words Jesus spoke while He Himself was on the cross. He used some of His last breaths to demonstrate a son's tender care for his mother by

A common temptation in the church is to hyper-focus on the nuclear family instead of embracing every member in every demographic as part of the family of God.

creating a new family for Mary, inviting one of His closest disciples to take care of her (John 19:25–27).

That tension can serve as a guard against idolatry within ourselves as well as within the church. One common personal temptation is to compare your real life, imperfect marriage, or family to the idealized images of marriage you may carry from either church or popular culture. A common temptation in the church is to hyper-focus on the nuclear family instead of embracing every member in every demographic as part of the family of God. There are more than one hundred and fifty "brother" or "brother and sister" references peppered throughout the New Testament epistles. Paul, Peter, and the other letter writers recognized that family was an essential way to describe our relationship with other believers.

Puritan-era preacher Jonathan Edwards offers some healthy perspective on family: "Fathers and mothers, husbands, wives, or children, or the company of earthly friends, are but shadows; but the enjoyment of God is the substance. These are but scattered beams; but God is the sun. These are but streams; but God is the fountain."[3]

When we're in the midst of building a marriage and raising children, we may long to try to hold on to sunbeams and dam the swiftly rushing stream of time.

Midlife is characterized by transition, and those transitions show themselves vividly against the backdrop of family life. Some changes, such as the birth of a grandchild, are joyous and welcome. Others, such as the death of a parent, are journeys into the valley of the shadow.

It is helpful to remember that transition is closely related to grief. All the markers that typically accompany grieving show themselves in times of transition: denial, anger, bargaining, depression, and acceptance.[4] Even a happy addition to the family tree means one chapter of life is ending and a new one is beginning.

What kind of changes might our families experience as we move into midlife, and how might they be forming us toward maturity? How can sages learn to discern how God might be at work in these changes?

CHANGE OF SEASON

I've lived in the Midwest most of my life. Though weather broadcasters sound shocked every year by the intensity of the temperature fluctuations and storms each spring and fall, I have learned to expect that one day the temperatures might be in the 70s, and the next, they might plummet into the 30s and we'll experience a freak blizzard in April.

The yearly weather roller coaster is a helpful picture to keep in mind as, during midlife, our families alter in ways that can feel as if we're doing loop-the-loops on an amusement park ride. Of course, a family is made up of always-changing human beings, so this life stage doesn't have a corner on the market when it comes to transition. However, many of the most challenging transitions to family life may cluster during this time of our lives. Here's a quick look at some of the biggies:

Dividing family: Divorce

Kate* and Matt* were committed Christians who tried everything from marriage conferences to individual and couples counseling, hoping to bring some stability to their fractious, unhappy union, but nothing ever seemed to change between them. Within a year of their youngest child heading off to college, the couple divorced.

Kate and Matt are part of a growing trend. According to the National Center for Family and Marriage Research, the divorce rate among American adults over age 50 has doubled since the 1990s.[5] Several studies have noted that the overall divorce rate among self-described evangelicals trends a bit higher than that of the general population, though some contest exactly how faith commitment in these studies was measured by researchers.[6] No matter who is doing the tabulating, it is safe to say that more of us are divorcing at midlife than in generations before us. Psychologist Vivian Diller noted, "Marriage has changed more over the past several decades than it has in thousands of years. Religious and societal pressures no longer provide the kind of adhesive power they once did when marriages ran into trouble."[7]

Kate and Matt's divorce followed the familiar narrative about couples staying together until the nest emptied "for the sake of the children." Addiction issues and/or abuse leads to many other divorces among older adults. In addition, as we begin to come to terms with the reality that our lives have a limited number of days and we've already lived a good number of them, some couples divorce as one or both parties decide they do not wish to live out the remainder of their years in an unhappy partnership.

Weary family: Marriage

When I talk with women who've been married for a couple of decades or more, I've rarely heard that midlife has been the easiest, most joyous period of many marriages. Though the newness of a "younger" marriage at midlife (by virtue of remarriage or marrying later) may temper somewhat the challenges those in long-term relationships face at this stage, stressors abound. Within the marriage, our sex lives may change as women head through perimenopause (more on this in chapter 6). Financial, family, and workplace pressures often pile on during these years. At some point—or, more likely, a bunch of points, lined up like an unending row of fenceposts leading into the future—marriage can feel like a hard slog.

Writer Belinda Luscombe describes it this way:

> Everyone who just got married is psyched about it. It's a new adventure they're embarking on with their best friend forever. Everyone who has been married for 50 years or more is psyched about it. They're living with their oldest friend, it's been a trip, totally worth it.
>
> But the people in the middle, they're, well—You know, they're *fine*. They perhaps didn't quite expect marriage to be as much work as it is. Not just the childcare and the housekeeping and the paying the bills, but the parts that are supposed to

be fun, the talking, the planning, the throwing a leg over. They had been led to believe it would feel easier, more natural. The thing about walking off into the sunset together is that then it gets dark and you're stumbling over each other.[8]

No family: Single

Aging without a network of support is a very real concern for many older singles.

At 51, Keisha* has never been married. "My twenties and thirties were marked by so much sorrow about my single state. I battled envy as I attended my friends' weddings, bought them baby gifts, and wrestled with my longing for God's gift of a mate and all I hoped would go with it: physical intimacy, companionship, spiritual partnership, and financial stability. As I moved into my forties, I came to terms with my singleness. (Well, most days, anyway!) I've poured my energy into building a good life and career for myself, spending time with friends, and developing my relationship with Christ. But now with both of my parents gone and my only sibling, a divorced brother, living across the country, I am staring down the prospect of aging alone, and it's more than a little concerning to me. I've never felt more single than I do right now."

Keisha's concern is shared by many of her divorced and widowed friends, particularly those who've never had children. According to senior advocacy organization AARP, one in five people over age 65 is an "elder orphan," someone aging alone without a family to oversee and advocate for their care. Twenty-three percent of boomers will be joining this group as they age, and there is no reason to believe these numbers won't stay steady or increase as Gen X moves toward retirement.[9]

Assisting family: Caring for parents, children, or grandchildren

ThePerennialGen.com, a website I cofounded with writer and editor Amanda Cleary Eastep, highlights a mix of writing from a variety of authors on midlife-related monthly themes. When we put out the call for posts about caregiving, we were overwhelmed by the number of submissions we received about the topic. The financial, time, and physical stresses of these responsibilities, and parent-child role reversals, often come at the same time our own kids are launching from the nest or having children of their own. Writer Connie Gochenauer told us:

> There is nothing unique about this season of mine as many women my age share these multiple roles. But when it is your own personal script, the emotions, changes, and role reversals are new, often heart-wrenching, and very complex. I sometimes wonder how the women before me have done this, and why I didn't pay better attention. The new roles can be somewhat confusing, and at times we find ourselves stepping on each other's lines.[10]

Caregiving concerns move in the opposite direction as well. There are over 2.6 million grandparents in this country raising their grandchildren.[11] And parents of some special needs children never face an empty nest. Instead, their daily life is very different from the daily life of peers their age. Their adult child may need a complex range of medical, social, vocational, or emotional support. These parents are navigating the challenges of each day while also trying to plan for a future when they will no longer be there to provide love, care, and advocacy for their child.

Shrinking family: Illness or death

I buried both of my parents by the time I was 48. The grief of saying goodbye to both of them at relatively young ages (64 and 68) was one of the gateways that led me into writing and thinking about midlife. Though it had been a long time since my parents were actively involved in protecting me as they did (to the best of their ability) when I was a young child, I didn't expect to carry the sense that there was now no one in my family who would buffer me from death. There was no older generation to pass away before it would be my turn.

Though it is true that no one knows the hour of their death (Eccl. 9:12), the expected order of things is that parents die before their children. I've known many parents who've lost beloved children, and the one painful truth that stands in every case is the notion that parents should never have to bury their children.

But when parents die before their children, many of us find tucked within our grief the painful existential reality that we may well be next in our families, and our children and grandchildren look to us to buffer death somehow for them. It is not a sign of faithlessness that we may be sucker-punched by this reality as we grieve the passing of our parents, even those with whom we may not have had a vibrant relationship. Beginning to contemplate our own passing is one of the big tasks of midlife. For me, the deaths of my parents moved that contemplation from the theoretical to the real, and moved me to pray Moses's words over my own life: "Teach us to number our days, that we may gain a heart of wisdom" (Ps. 90:12).

At midlife, the decline in health of one (or both) partners in a marriage will also change the dynamics in a family. My long-time prayer partner Meg walked alongside her beloved husband Marty as he dealt with unpredictable waves of life-threatening health crises for several years. She served as medical appointment scheduler, wound dresser, prescription refiller, and primary support system. The caregiving responsibilities weighed heavily on her at times, but she balanced them with a grateful "At least he's still here."

And then one day, he wasn't.

She was in her early sixties when she became a widow after more than four decades of marriage. In Marty's absence, Meg is now living the reality of the words C. S. Lewis penned after the death of his wife Joy Davidman: "Her absence is like the sky, spread over everything."[12] That sky envelops not only Meg, but her children and grandchildren and the extended family. They cannot go back to who they were when Marty was alive.

Stretching family: Relationships with adult children

Many of our children reach adulthood at the same time we hit middle age, though there are some of us having children well into our forties. (I became a grandmother the same year my sister-in-law, who is a year older than me, had her last child.)

But historically, midlife is the time during which our nest empties and we renegotiate our relationships with our young adult children. There is enough material in this category to be an entirely different book. Even the nicest version of these transitional years isn't free of big emotions for parent and child alike.

Author Jamie Janosz gave these words of gentle coaching in a blog post for ThePerennialGen.com to other parents facing the launch of a young adult child: "You will feel—at moments—like you can't. But you can and will survive it by focusing on the end. And by remembering to breathe. This is what you have been preparing your child for—this is why you've studied hard and raised them right. And really . . . you don't want a 40-year-old hermit living in your basement, right?"[13]

However, these years are also full of unexpected surprises when it comes to our kids—and not all of them are joyful. They may make decisions we may not agree with. They may become involved in relationships we can't celebrate. And some discover our children are no longer interested in living the faith with which they were raised.

In his book *Generation Ex-Christian*, Drew Dyck lists several different categories of contemporary prodigals:

- Postmodern leavers—This group leaves because as they perceive the church, it has been enmeshed in conservative politics or displays a lack of compassion for the poor and marginalized.[14]
- Recoilers—This group moves away from faith because they've experienced spiritual or physical abuse from a church leader, group, or Christian family member.[15]
- Modern leavers—Like their postmodern kin, these leavers have tried Christianity and found it wanting, but their objections are connected intellectually to the popular atheism of Richard Dawkins and Sam Harris.[16]

- Neo-pagans—This group of prodigals embraces their "spiritual but not religious" identity with a mix of everything from wicca to New Age, sometimes with a splash of Christianity mixed in for good measure.[17]
- Rebels—These are the classic "younger brother" prodigals marked by hedonism in lifestyle. Some rebel in search of the next party, others because they've decided Christianity seems repressive.[18]
- Drifters—Dyck believes this group is the largest in number of all the prodigals: "These are the slow-motion leavers. They don't exit in sudden spasms of skepticism or rebellion. Instead they leave gradually, almost imperceptibly."[19]

For some parents, a prodigal child is an introduction to Stage 4, the "dark night of the soul" of our own faith journey.

For some parents, a prodigal child is an introduction to Stage 4, the "dark night of the soul" of our own faith journey. For parents of leavers, learning to navigate the relational conflict emerging from our sadness, worry, or disappointment over a prodigal's choices is a complex process that calls for growth in humility, love, and surrender to God.

Expanding family: Grandchildren and in-laws

Our family circle stretches at midlife as our adult children begin to create their own families. Even the most joyous of unions can be stressors as the children from two different families begin a new life together. I knew one person who used a multi-year calendar that tracked when each of her children, their spouses, and their grandchildren would or wouldn't be attending Christmas and Thanksgiving gatherings at her home as each balanced time with the spouse's extended family.

A complicated calendar highlights the oft-complex nature of what it can mean to forge a new relationship, not only with a new son-in-law or daughter-in-law, but with our now married child. If those dynamics are difficult, they can be exponentially more so once children enter the picture. However, new babies bring with them much joy and a whole new set of lessons for grandparents.

Scripture tells us that grandchildren are a blessing that extends and enriches the family circle: "Children's children are a crown to the aged, and parents are the pride of their children" (Prov. 17:6). I became a grandmother in the midst of both of my own parents' deaths. Seeing the toothless smile of my newborn grandson beaming up at me as I cradled him in my arms made me recognize that standing on the top rung of the ladder of my family was weighted with a new kind of responsibility in prayer and legacy creation—as well as a new kind of joy.

FROM TEACHER TO LEARNER

When we're children, the family is a primary shaper of our identity. It is our first classroom as we learn to relate to God and others. As we move into adulthood and many of us form households and families of our own, we assume the mantle of responsibility for training up our children in the way they should go in their own journeys with God (Prov. 22:6). That mantle is a weighty one, but it is not one we're meant to wear at midlife and beyond in the same way we did during the first half of our lives. In addition, our other family relationships—with our spouses, parents, the partners of our children, our grandchildren,

As we move into our second adulthood, the shifts that happen in our families can be used by God to reintroduce us to the truth that we're first and foremost apprentices, not headmasters.

and members of our local church—call for our transformation and growth as our families change shape through time.

As we move into our second adulthood, the shifts that happen in our families can be used by God to reintroduce us to the truth that we're first and foremost apprentices, not headmasters.

When I was a young parent, I assumed that the mandate God gave in Deuteronomy 6:4–9 to pass on my faith to the next generation had a uni-directional focus: the parent is the teacher of their child. However, most of the imperatives in the passage assume intergenerational learning. We're to live our apprenticeship together by talking about God's commands when we're at home and out in the world, when we rest and when we work, always seeking to weave every facet of our lives into His. Apprenticeship encompasses all of life, and the stresses and strengths of family life is a primary and always-changing classroom. Sages-in-training are students.

Apprenticeship in family can take on many different forms. A divorce can lead us to new ways of depending on God. Marriage at midlife requires us to recalibrate and reinvest in this primary relationship. Singlehood brings new questions and challenges as we begin to confront our own mortality. Caregiving asks us to renegotiate parent-child relationships. In addition, some find at midlife that their own long-dormant family-of-origin issues surface in the midst of the changes they're experiencing. It's not an accident.

Loss changes us. We find ourselves contemplating our own passing after parents die. The passing of a spouse disrupts dreams we may have shared about the way our final years would unfold in the company of a cherished companion. Launching our children requires us to learn to relinquish them, and ourselves, to the care of our heavenly Father. And as our children make their own choices, forge new relationships, or start families of their own, our family stretches into new shapes we may never have imagined.

God uses early family life to form us, and the shifts of midlife to re-form us. The apprenticeship custom designed for each of us by our heavenly Father is specific to our unique situation. The Holy Spirit—the Promised One whom Jesus described as our helper, companion, and guide (John 14:16–17, 26)—is an always-present tutor in our lives.

When we're disoriented by the changes in our family structure, two evergreen practices may help steady us:

The first is asking, "Please reveal to me what You want me to learn, Lord." He doesn't hand us His entire lesson plan for our lives in response, but the request positions us to recognize the ways in which He's at work and to respond to Him in obedience. The New Living Translation of Matthew 7:7 captures the ongoing, persistent action for which Jesus called on the part of the seeker:[20] "Keep on asking, and you will receive what you ask for. Keep on seeking, and you will find. Keep on knocking, and the door will be opened to you." Even if darkness, sorrow, or disorientation seems to muffle His answer, knocking and continuing to knock is an expression of hope in the One who has His hand on the doorknob and has promised to welcome us in.

The second practice is gratitude. Our Father has placed us in a physical family and guided us to a spiritual family. Those places of belonging may carry with them memories of significant loss or pain. It may not seem possible to thank God for those searing experiences, but committing to express gratitude for the good gifts He has given you is another orienting practice.

Dr. Harvey Simon of Harvard Medical School noted:

> Gratitude helps people feel more positive emotions, relish good experiences, improve their health, deal with adversity, and build strong relationships.... They can apply it to the past (retrieving positive memories and being thankful for elements of childhood or past blessings), the present (not taking good fortune for granted as it comes), and the future (maintaining a hopeful and optimistic attitude).[21]

Gratitude is good for everyone, but for believers, it is more than just a positive mental health practice. There is a Giver who deserves our thanks. James 1:17 tells us, "Every good and perfect gift is from above, coming down from the Father of the heavenly lights, who does not change like shifting shadows."

During a time in our lives filled with family transitions that may feel like shape-shifting shadows, becoming sage may mean renewing and deepening the habits we likely learned in early childhood—the practices of saying "please" and "thank you" to our heavenly Father.

Recognize that these practices won't magically mute the discomfort of change. They won't expedite the journey through the grief of saying goodbye to who our family once was . . . or even who we wish they'd become in the future. But both habits can steady us as we learn acceptance at midlife for who our family is here and now.

FOR INDIVIDUAL REFLECTION

1. Are there joyful ways in which your family is being reshaped during this period of your life? If so, what are they? Are there sorrowful ways your family is changing? Offer your responses to God in a prayer of thanksgiving and/or lament. If you're looking for inspiration, begin with Scripture. Examples of psalms of thanksgiving include Psalms 32, 100, and 136. Some psalms of lament include Psalms 44, 80, and 90.

2. What are your greatest fears when you think about your family? Confess those fears to God and ask for His help in moving from fear to love in those areas. What would it look like to be free of those fears?

3. Meditate on Psalm 145:4: "One generation commends your works to another; they tell of your mighty acts." To which works of God can you give testimony? How might you show and tell of God's works to a challenging family member?

FOR GROUP CONVERSATION

1. In what ways do you see "family as idol" normalized or celebrated in Christian culture? In your own local church?

2. How does your church provide spiritual or practical support for those facing changes in their family status due to:

- Divorce?
- Marriage?
- Aging and dying parents?
- Illness or death of a spouse?

- Changing relationships with adult children?
- The advent of grandchildren and/or in-laws?

If there are gaps, consider asking for input from those currently facing these changes, as well as those who've faced them in the past. What do they need most from your congregation?

3. Many midlife parents are dealing with adult children who have walked away from the faith. How can you make space to hear their stories and find ways to pray for them and their children on an ongoing basis? This might include a general prayer during a Sunday service, a regular time of prayer in a small group, or even gathering parents of prodigals for an evening of prayer where they can share one another's burdens.

Becoming sage happens as the relational shifts of midlife reshape our families and we move from the teacher to the learner role.

CHAPTER 5

FOREVER FRIENDS

*Some relationships endure, others fade,
and others begin*

It's the last night of church youth camp in 1993. Cricket song echoes in the pines outside the chapel. There is a moment of silent prayer after the speaker has given the final message, and everyone in the room is feeling especially close to one another and to God. In that moment, the worship leader steps up to the mic and begins strumming the familiar chords to Michael W. Smith's 1987 CCM megahit, "Friends." Two hundred teens spontaneously link arms and sing the promise that they'll be friends forever because the Lord is Lord of them all.

A few of those camp-birthed friendships may last a lifetime. But as we grow and change throughout adulthood, other "forever friendships" will fade.

Like many women, I had a stable circle of friends throughout my child-rearing years. My pals and I compared notes about potty training, shuttled kids to one another's homes for play dates, and cheered, coached, and prayed for one another as we raised our kids through elementary and high school. Some of our kids probably sang Michael W. Smith's song in youth group, but I believed the lyrics were equally applicable to those of us who'd spent so much time together while raising our kids. I never doubted that our shared experiences and, in most cases, our shared faith would be enough to cement our friendships for life.

Shifts at midlife threw us out of sync with one another. Our kids scattered. Some headed to college, others into the workforce or the military. Meanwhile, a couple of my mom friends relocated once their nests were empty. Others put new energy into their careers. Still others saw their marriages come to an end. For a while, it seemed the easiest way to deal with the new distance in these relationships was to make excuses for it ("How did we get so busy? Let's get a date on the calendar ASAP!") or to try to pretend nothing had changed. Eventually, I realized I might have overestimated some of these relationships a tad. A number of those I'd included in my circle of BFFs had really been church and parenting coworkers.

At midlife, many of us discover we're downsizing and moving into a brand-new neighborhood, so to speak. The relocation strips us of the things that formed our network of relationships back in the old neighborhood of our twenties and thirties: children's activities or the drive to find meaning in a career. This new life location can be lonely. No one I know is riding in a red convertible with her empty-nester "gal pals" singing along to oldies while heading to a beach house weekend. Most of us aren't looking for gal pals, anyway. We're simply looking for a few friends in our new neighborhood.[1]

Women have shared stories with me from their new neighborhoods. I've heard descriptions of anchoring relationships that have continued since childhood. I've heard reports of new friendships blooming in the soil of life change.

But I've also heard many, many accounts of loneliness. Women have shared with me their struggles to find and maintain friendships: "I've moved to a new town, and struggle to break into already established social groups in my church and community," "I've been so busy caring for my aging parents that I haven't had time to invest in friendships," or "I've followed the standard advice to get involved in new ways at church or in the community to make new friends, and none of these relationships go beyond the surface acquaintance stage."

The lament in these stories highlights how important friendship is. Our friends sustain, support, and strengthen us. At midlife, as our nest empties and our family relationships shift, our friendships can take on new importance in our lives.

THE FELLOWSHIP OF FRIENDS

God has built us for relationship with Him and with one another. Even before Adam in the garden had any notion that he was alone, God responded with Eve, saying, "It is not good for the man to be alone. I will make a helper suitable for him" (Gen. 2:18). Though we often hear this verse quoted in the context of marriage, the truth it contains extends to all human relationships. Friends notice and delight in what is good in us. Those essential relationships teach us how to grow in love for God and our neighbors, according to thirteenth-century theologian Thomas Aquinas: "In order that man may do well, whether in the works of the active life, or in those of the contemplative life, he needs the fellowship of friends."[2]

C. S. Lewis reminds us that healthy friendship helps us be better, wiser humans:

> Friendship is not a reward for our discrimination and good taste in finding one another out. It is the instrument by which God reveals to each the beauties of all the others. They are no greater than the beauties of a thousand other men; by Friendship God opens our eyes to them. They are, like all beauties, derived from Him, and then, in a good Friendship, increased by Him through the Friendship itself, so that it is His instrument for creating as well as for revealing. At this feast it is He who has spread the board and it is He who has chosen the guests.[3]

We do not select our families, but those we call our friends reflects a powerful chosen love. Scripture highlights unforgettable friendships like that of Ruth and Naomi or David and Jonathan. We recognize great friendships in literary classics like that of Sam and Frodo in the Lord of the Rings series or Anne Shirley and Diana Barry in *Anne of Green Gables*.

Friends are people who cherish one another, sticking "closer than a brother" (Prov. 18:24). The best kind of friendships create safe zones that allow us to reveal the truth about ourselves (Prov. 27:5–6). Friends provide mutual support (Eccl. 4:9–10).

Scripture also reveals that one friend can betray another with the knowledge they've gained from relational closeness, as we see in the case of Judas's stunning disloyalty to Jesus. And yet, as Judas was on his way to betray Jesus, Jesus spoke these words to His disciples: "Greater love has no one than this: to lay down one's life for one's friends. You are my friends if you do what I command. I no longer call you servants, because a servant does not know his master's business. Instead, I have called you friends, for everything that I learned from my Father I have made known to you" (John 15:13–15).

This kind of friendship Jesus offers us is marked by perfect love expressed in sacrifice and intimacy. All of our other healthy friendships can reflect a measure of that love.

ONE CAN BE A VERY LONELY NUMBER

Lack of friendships in our lives carries with it a cost far higher than most of us may even realize. Loneliness, that sense of isolation or abandonment, is a serious issue with far-reaching physical, social, and spiritual consequences. You can be lonely in a family, a church, or a crowd. However, more and more of us find ourselves living alone in America. The *Wall Street Journal* reports that about eight million Americans over age 50 do not have a spouse or children, a key source of companionship and support as we age. Forecasters expect this number to grow in coming decades.[4]

However, living alone is not the only indicator of loneliness. Researchers in one longitudinal study of more than 1,600 adults over 60 noted, "43% of the study population weren't necessarily living alone . . . The link between loneliness and poor health held even after the researchers took into account living situation, depression, and a wide range of other factors, suggesting that feelings of loneliness or isolation might independently damage health in some way."[5]

Award-winning reporter Barbara Bradley Haggerty poured herself into her career during the first half of her life. But at midlife, she discovered her focus on her career left her relationally impoverished. She said,

> I once believed *having* friends was a luxury. Now I know that *losing* friends can be lethal. Feeling lonely and isolated, no matter what your age, will shorten your life as much as smoking fifteen cigarettes a day. It destroys your body as effectively as alcoholism. It is twice as lethal as obesity. Maintaining relationships with friends, family, or work colleagues increases your odds of survival by 50 percent.[6]

Loneliness is a part of our human experience, but it is one that Jesus understands deeply. The prophecy in Isaiah 53 about the coming Messiah describes Him as One who knows what it is to be rejected and alone: "He was despised and rejected by mankind, a man of suffering, and familiar with pain. Like one from whom people hide their faces he was despised, and we held him in low esteem" (Isa. 53:3). Throughout His ministry, Jesus dealt with character assassination and rejection from religious leaders. The fulfillment of Isaiah's words about Jesus were most poignantly seen in the desolation He experienced while on the cross. His ragged cry in Mark 15:34 of "My God, my God, why have you forsaken me?" enfolds our experiences of abandonment in His self-giving love for us.

There is comfort for us in discovering ways we're not abandoned in our loneliness. And at midlife, when loneliness often becomes more insistent in our lives, learning to press into God's presence is how we experience that comfort. We face the temptation to find a way to ease our discomfort by anesthetizing it (with food, shopping, drinking, drug abuse) or hiding from it in busyness.

Pressing in means not running from it but facing our loneliness head on. The process is about more than attempting to bring to mind what God's Word says about His promises to be with us always, though it is essential to remember that Scripture anchors and directs us into truth. Because loneliness is not merely a cognitive experience, coming to God just as you are also means bringing all of who you are—your aching heart, your sense of physical distance from others, and your hurting emotions—before Him.

Not all alone-ness is lonely. Time spent solely in the company of God in chosen solitude is a classic spiritual discipline that can deepen our roots in Him as well as helping us befriend ourselves. Henri Nouwen said:

> To live a spiritual life we must first find the courage to enter into the desert of our loneliness and to change it by gentle and persistent efforts into a garden of solitude.... The movement from loneliness to solitude, however, is the beginning of any spiritual life because it is the movement from the restless senses to the restful spirit, from the outward-reaching cravings to the inward-reaching search, from the fearful clinging to the fearless play.[7]

Solitude can be a challenge to both introverts and extroverts. Those who relish time alone don't necessarily have an "edge" over extroverts, who are refueled by time in the company of others. As Nouwen notes, solitude is far richer and more spiritually challenging than simply adjusting to being alone. It bears intention of the same kind we see in Jesus' stealing away in order to commune with His Father (Luke 4:1–13; 5:16; 6:12–13; 22:39–46). Solitude is a healthy practice that can allow you to dial into your relationship with God without an audience or a to-do list. Paradoxically, solitude can also help to reframe and repurpose the experience of loneliness, strengthening us to re-engage afresh with the world around us.

MAKE NEW FRIENDS, KEEP THE OLD

Long before Michael W. Smith penned "Friends," Welsh poet Joseph Parry wrote the poem "New Friends and Old Friends." The Girl Scouts used some of this poem for the lyrics of a song beloved by the organization.[8] The first lines will be familiar to anyone who has ever sold a box of Thin Mints: "Make new friends / but keep the old / one is silver / and the other gold."

At midlife, how can we cultivate those silver and gold relationships in our lives? Some of us are blessed with a few long-time relationships that are comfortable, steady, and grounded in shared history. The challenge with these relationships is continuing to find time to connect in the midst of the busyness of daily life. The trust built into the history of these friendships allows many of these relationships to absorb separations of time and distance. Those in true gold friendships are able to pick up right where they left off, whether a few days or many months have elapsed. I am blessed to have a few golden friends in my life, and with each passing year, I am more aware than ever what a treasure they are to me. There's nothing like having someone in your life who knew you "when," and still loves you now.

However, as I noted at the beginning of this chapter, not all old friendships make the transition into midlife without some alchemy that changes the nature of the relationship. This friendship may reveal itself as less than the pure gold you once assumed it was. That revelation doesn't negate the worth of the relationship, nor does it necessarily mean that at some point in the future there may not be a fresh rekindling of it, if only for occasional catch-up visits. Recognizing and grieving those changes is a necessary journey toward healthy acceptance of what the relationship is at this point of your life. In some cases, that reassessment may result in a good "define the relationship" conversation with your friend. In other cases, it may be wiser to simply embrace the current relationship without trying to dig through the past in hopes of recapturing an earlier closeness.

While the Serenity Prayer (attributed to sources ranging from Augustine to Reinhold Niebuhr) has application in many areas of our lives, it definitely offers a helpful spiritual grid through which to prayerfully discern how to approach changing friendships: "God, grant me the serenity to accept the things I cannot change, courage to change the things I can, and wisdom to know the difference."

My life is richer because of a handful of old gold friends in my life, as well as some wonderful newer "silver" friends I've made in

Remaining open to making new friendships at midlife comes with a cost.

recent years. I may not yet share history with these new friends, but they are excellent, diverse companions God has used to teach, strengthen, and encourage me at this stage of my life. (I pray I bring that same sort of energy to these friends as well!)

Remaining open to making new friendships at midlife comes with a cost, however. At this stage of our lives, holding space for the possibility of a new relationship will call on us to risk some comfort and pride. We may risk reaching out to a potential friend only to discover that person isn't interested in reciprocating. Not everyone will make space in their social orbit for us. We won't click with some people.

Vanessa* wrote me to say she was still struggling to find new friends after more than two years in a new town. She'd done all the "right" things: volunteering at church, joining a book club at the library, taking a class at the community college, and working hard to get to know her neighbors. "Am I always going to be 'the new girl' here?" she asked.

I didn't have an easy answer for Vanessa. I affirmed that her disheartening circumstances were not a measure of her worth or value as a person and empathized with the discouragement she was feeling. There are no quick remedies to this problem. During the course of our conversation, we brainstormed some strategies to combat her loneliness. Some of those strategies included: continuing to find ways to stay appropriately connected with friends in her former hometown for emotional support; seeking out new opportunities to serve alongside others on projects or ministries she's passionate about both at church and in her new community; praying and journaling to process her emotions and desires; and seeking out a seasoned spiritual director who could come alongside her and help her discern how God might be at work in this difficult time in her life.

When my kids were little, I could bring them to a playground and they'd bond instantly with the other kids there, forming ad hoc teams for games of tag. There have been times as an adult when I've been the "new girl" at church, wishing someone would tag me and invite me to be a part of their team.

Don't we all want that very thing? The spiritual challenge before those who are a part of comfortable, established social circles is to seek to keep that circle open to welcome a new friend into the group. Long-time groups of friends have their own internal culture and rhythms of interaction. But wherever possible—say, at church, at work, or in a neighborhood—doing what you can to keep a circle open is a way to express the love of God not only to a "new girl," but as a way of encouraging growth in emotional and relational maturity for other members of the group. Becoming sage can be contagious in these settings.

WALK WITH ME

There is one form of silver friendship that can flourish in the rich soil of our second-half lives: mentoring. A mentor is a more experienced person who coaches a less experienced person in a relationship that is focused on passing on specific skills or knowledge.

Modern mentor-mentee relationships happen in business and in the arts.

But they've been a part of the church's call to apprenticeship from the beginning. We see this reflected in Paul's instruction to Titus about how older women are to mentor the younger women in the church community:

> Likewise, teach the older women to be reverent in the way they live, not to be slanderers or addicted to much wine, but to teach what is good. Then they can urge the younger women to love their husbands and children, to be self-controlled and pure, to be busy at home, to be kind, and to be subject to their husbands, so that no one will malign the word of God. (Titus 2:3–5)

Though this passage calls upon older women to disciple their younger sisters in faith, the relationship was never meant to be a one-way street. Older women were expected to be students, too. As they learned sound doctrine, they were able to work out its implications and applications in the living lab of their daily lives as they interacted with those they were discipling.

When rigidly prescribed roles, forms, and curriculum are superimposed on what is meant to be a relationship that reflects the way faith was designed by God to be transmitted—through His life shared together—discipleship starts looking like a project. Or worse, a product.

It is meant to be a friendship. And this kind of friendship is not limited only to those older women who appear to be spiritual success stories. Younger women are looking for mentors willing to be authentic about their failures and ongoing struggles to work out their salvation "with fear and trembling" (Phil. 2:12).

I'd been working part time for a few months at a campus bookstore at a Christian college more than a decade ago when one of my young coworkers, a student, asked me to mentor her. She knew my struggles, flaws, and failings because I'd shared bits of them in conversation as we worked alongside one another shelving dusty textbooks, just as she'd shared parts of hers with me. Though I was "the older woman," I was not in a position of authority over her. We were simply coworkers with identical job descriptions who'd become friends. The friendship took on a more intentional focus after her Titus 2 ask. Together we sought to learn what reverent, self-controlled faithfulness looked like in our lives over varied and regular hangout time during the rest of her years at the school and occasional catch-up conversations nowadays.[9]

These apprenticeship-themed friendships grow best out of shared time together. You may find a place of connection with a younger friend at church, through volunteering at a parachurch ministry such as MOPS or a community-based Bible study, or through your existing network of relationships.

As we move into the second half of our lives and consider the friends we've had, the friends we lack, and the friendships we hope to form moving forward, those becoming sage recognize that whether for a specific season or for a lifetime, God uses each one of our relationships to form us for eternity.

FOR INDIVIDUAL REFLECTION

1. List the most meaningful long-term friendships you've had during the first half of your life. Have these relationships changed over time? If so, how? How have these relationships formed you?

2. While Scripture offers us the stories of friendships like Ruth and Naomi or David and Jonathan, it also highlights a close partnership between Paul and Barnabas that results in division in Acts 15:36–41. Read the passage and contemplate the reasons for the separation between the two friends. Do you believe the division between the two was the result of sin on the part of one or both men? Or could it have been the result of growth?

3. Remember a time in your life when you have experienced deep loneliness, or consider the loneliness you may be feeling at the present time. Pour out your true feelings in a psalm (or series of psalms) to God. Don't hold back! Be still and ask what God might be saying in response to those prayers.

FOR GROUP CONVERSATION

1. Reflect on the friendships you see within your church. Do they function as "closed circle" cliques? Why do you say so?

2. What is the unlikeliest friendship you've ever had? What made it so? How has God used it in your life?

3. Who has mentored you? Describe that relationship. How does your congregation approach mentoring? Consider inviting some people currently serving as mentors and mentees (perhaps

in two separate meetings) to describe their relationship. What might you learn from these conversations that would allow your leadership team to find ways to better nurture a culture of friendship in your church?

Becoming sage relationally includes learning to be alone with God, leaning into times of deep loneliness, remaining open to new connections, and nurturing or renegotiating old friendships in the context of the security we have in our friendship with God.

CHAPTER 6

GLORIFY GOD WITH *THIS* BODY?

*Aging bodies are far more than disposable
containers for souls*

W hen I was in sixth grade, the teachers divided us by gender
for a series of "special" classes. The boys got a scientific
explanation about what was about to happen to their bodies and
some general cautions about protecting themselves from sexually transmitted diseases. The girls were treated to a viewing of a
clinical movie about puberty, then handed a packet of mattress-
sized sanitary napkins and a granny-sized elastic belt to use with
those pads once we began menstruating.

Many people groups have coming-of-age customs, like the
quinceañera celebration in Latin American culture that marks a
fifteen-year-old girl's transition into womanhood or the bar and
bat mitzvah celebrations that signify that Jewish boys and girls

(respectively) have come to an age of spiritual accountability. That series of special classes at my elementary school was about as far from a rite of passage as could be, but the awkward information download and the, uh . . . lovely parting gifts for us girls . . . were an acknowledgment that new things were happening to us all.

I think men and women over forty or so could use a class of some kind about our changing bodies at midlife. Maybe they'd make women return a box of sanitary napkins during this class, a ritual acknowledging that we're in the final approach to menopause. Perhaps as an acknowledgment of their gradually declining testosterone levels after age 30, men could name and claim one physical activity they did during their teens and twenties (such as moving an upright piano up two flights of stairs with a buddy) that may not be such a good idea as they age. The changes taking place in our bodies at midlife and beyond can be just as confusing as they were at the onset of puberty.

The physiological changes at midlife tend to be more dramatic for women as their childbearing years draw to a conclusion. After a woman has ceased to have a menstrual period for a full year, she's considered to be in menopause. The average age of menopause in the United States is 51.[1] Perimenopause, the process by which our bodies move into menopause, can last from between four and ten years prior to that.[2] Some of us move through these years of transition without a hiccup, and others experience sometimes debilitating symptoms including irregular periods, mood swings, lower sex drive, hot flashes, and difficulty sleeping.

If we are created in God's image, the cessation of menses is as much a part of His good design for women as is our eye color. Had death not entered the equation at the fall in the garden of

Eden, perhaps menopause as part of the natural aging process wouldn't exist or would look entirely different than what we experience now. Any discussion of spiritual formation at midlife must begin with the foundational truth that both women and men are crafted in the image of God. He created us above all the rest of His creation to carry out His purposes on earth (Gen. 1:28) and live in communion with Him and each other (Gen. 2:24). The fall marred, but does not erase, the beautiful reality that each one of us as individuals—and all of us together as humanity—carry our Maker's imprint.

If God calls us to glorify Him with our bodies (1 Cor. 6:19–20), then He has a purpose for those marvelous bodies at every physical life stage and within every limitation.

During the second century, Irenaeus of Lyons fought the heresy of Gnosticism that threatened to take root in the church. This heresy elevated the spirit above the body and physical world in importance. Irenaeus wrote, "The glory of God is man fully alive."[3] Jesus, fully God and fully man, came to us in a human body because every part of us—heart, soul, mind, and body—is in need of the redemption He wrought for us. His bodily resurrection underscores the reality that His salvation encompasses the whole of who we are.

Today in many churches, we hear a low-level form of modern Gnosticism in the way we talk about salvation. When we describe faith in terms of mental assent to facts about God or we equate our ecstatic emotions after a powerful revival service as a measure of His nearness, we feed the erroneous narrative that the spirit is more important than the body. In addition, well-meaning attempts to counteract our culture's approach to sexuality have resulted in messaging in some streams of the church that bodies—in particular, women's bodies—are tempting, dangerous, and bad. Theologian N. T. Wright spoke about the way in which we "silo" and divide our hearts, souls, minds, and bodies in ways God never intended:

> Each and every aspect of the human being is addressed by God, is claimed by God, is loved by God, and can respond to God. It is not the case that God, as it were, sneaks in to the human being through one aspect in order to influence or direct the rest. Every step in that direction is a step towards the downgrading of the body . . . And that downgrading has demonstrably gone hand in hand, in various Christian movements, with either a careless disregard for the created order or a careless disregard for bodily morality. Or both.[4]

I've seen what it can look like to value the whole person in ministries that serve under-resourced communities, such as Breakthrough Urban Ministries (breakthrough.org) in Chicago. Providing community care that includes healthy food options, job training, violence prevention, housing help, tutoring, and more are all part of the organization's proclamation of the gospel. Breakthrough's un-siloed approach to ministry is distributed between heart, soul, mind, and strength. While a small congregation may not be able to do everything a large ministry like Breakthrough does, I've appreciated the efforts of a couple of churches I've known to ensure they've created meaningful connections to community resources such as free dental clinics, counseling, short-term housing, crisis pregnancy centers, and food pantries.

We'd all do well to remember that our bodies are not just

disposable containers for our souls but are integral as we journey toward holy maturity: "Do you not know that your bodies are temples of the Holy Spirit, who is in you, whom you have received from God? You are not your own; you were bought at a price. Therefore honor God with your bodies" (1 Cor. 6:19–20).

The results of a recent study published in the *Journal of Religion and Health* that was conducted by researchers at Biola University revealed that religious beliefs shaped the way in which respondents viewed their bodies. Summarizing the study, *Christianity Today* magazine writer David Briggs noted that people of faith who viewed their bodies as sinful or merely a disposable container for the soul carried shame about their bodies. On the other hand, those who'd embraced the teaching that their bodies were created by God and that God could be glorified through the body had a grateful, healthy appreciation for their physical selves.[5]

Those who teach through a filter of shame about the body in hopes of counterbalancing the overheated focus on sex in our culture may do so out of a desire to promote purity and chastity. However, that filter communicates that our bodies are problems to be conquered rather than being a reflection of the One who made them—and that includes everything from our appearance, sexual desires, and ongoing physical changes that mark our passage through life on earth. Grounded scriptural teaching about the goodness of our bodies, as well as warnings and consequences highlighting the ways in which our bodies can lead us to sin, are both essential to healthy spiritual formation. A solid scriptural foundation that rebuts some of these popular poor ideas can guide us in the midst of midlife changes in our fertility, intimate lives, physical appearance, and health at midlife.

THE END IS THE BEGINNING

I can count on one hand the number of women I've known who slipped effortlessly into menopause. Many others have experiences like that of one of my friends at the height of perimenopause who had periods that lasted two weeks, stopped for a week, started again for a few days, then skipped three months before returning to start the roller coaster all over again.

I'd always been prone to migraines that seemed to accompany my menstrual cycles, but they became more intense, frequent, and debilitating during perimenopause. A sympathetic doctor told me he expected the miserable headaches to mostly disappear once I hit menopause. Thanks be to God, the doctor was right. Menopause for me brought physical relief to years of migraine misery.

But the physical relief I felt was shadowed by a sense of loss. Kara,* the parent of three teens, told me she was surprised at how deeply she mourned the end of her childbearing years. "It's not that I wish I could have another baby at this point of my life, but there's something so final about this. This chapter of my life is at an end." Kara added that she felt as though something was slipping away that was at the core of her feminine identity. I have felt the same way myself.

I received this correspondence about the experience of menopause from a never-married woman[6] in her fifties:

> When I went through menopause, I didn't just have a "sense" of loss, there was a true loss of never having a child. And since there is no childbirth in heaven, then never is really never **ever**. I know God will make up for every loss I've had on

earth. I know there will be no sorrow in the life to come. My head knows this, but my heart can't seem to comprehend the idea, so my loss is different than that of one who has married and had children. I just want to know that people like me are seen, recognized, validated by the Church.

Menopause can usher some of us into the perplexing world of the "dark night of the soul" of Stage 4 faith. Facing and processing those feelings of loss and disorientation can be a journey several years in duration, tracing the path our body is following as we move toward and into menopause. Editors James Nelson and Sandra Longfellow noted that this physical transition calls on women to "come to terms with their procreative history, to grieve their losses. . . . The graceful opportunities menopause offers women are new self-understanding, new interpretations of the meanings of their lifelong sexuality, and movement from their old life into . . . what anthropologist Margaret Mead once called 'post-menopausal zest.'"[7]

We can see elements in the biblical account of Sarai of this process of mourning the past, reframing the present, and living a generative life with "post-menopausal zest." When we first meet Sarai in Genesis 12, she's been infertile for her entire adult life and may well have been in menopause. She was likely in her sixties at this point but was still a physically attractive woman (Gen. 12:10–13). As the years continued to pass, God's promise to her husband Abram of heirs as numerous as the stars in the skies weighed heavily on Sarai's soul, perhaps amplifying her own sorrow at her barrenness. She comes up with a plan to give her husband a child by giving her maid Hagar as a wife to Abram (Gen. 16:1–4).

God blessed the child of Hagar and Abram (Gen. 16:7–16), but again underscored His promise to Abram to give him a child with his treasured wife Sarai, giving the pair new names. Sarai ("princess") became Sarah ("my princess"), a name fit for the matriarch of a clan too numerous to count (Gen. 17). Abraham, 99, and Sarai, 89, acted in marital intimacy in response to this word from God, and a year later their miracle child was born. Sarah's awestruck, zesty words echo across time to us today: "God has brought me laughter, and everyone who hears about this will laugh with me . . . . Who would have said to Abraham that Sarah would nurse children? Yet I have borne him a son in his old age" (Gen. 21:6–7).

The message here isn't that we are all supposed to become first-time mothers in our nineties. Sarai/Sarah's story highlights the fact that on the other side of menopause, our lives are meant to continue to grow in faith, beauty, and nurture. Our changing, sage-ing bodies are essential to that growth.

SEX ON THE OTHER SIDE OF MENOPAUSE

The web is full of articles touting the health benefits of remaining sexually active as we age, along with lots of tips on how to keep the flame burning. And a lot of us remain interested in sex, even as we move into the final years of our lives. The University of Michigan's 2018 National Poll on Healthy Aging found that 40 percent of respondents over age 65 were still sexually active.[8] Our sex lives may not look quite like the youthful passion captured in the Song of Songs in our Bible, but our desire for connection and intimacy is a gift from God that exists at every stage of our lives.

It's a normal, healthy desire to wish to stoke the fire in a long-term marriage or forge a vibrant intimate relationship with a new mate if an earlier marriage ends in death or divorce. Media images of fit boomer marathoners and actresses who are "sexy at 60"

Our sex lives may not look quite like the youthful passion captured in the Song of Songs in our Bible, but our desire for connection and intimacy is a gift from God that exists at every stage of our lives.

have replaced the last generation's norm of genderless, thick-waisted, polyester-clad grandparents playing Bingo in the retirement home. We're living longer, with a greater understanding of diet, exercise, and medical treatments for conditions that used to slow us down.

Today, we have access to those sexual enhancement drugs such as Viagra for men and Osphena for women that promise to keep us forever young. For many, these products have lived up to their promises to enhance intimacy—countering the effects of other medications, alleviating sexual performance anxiety, and extending sexually active years beyond what most of our forebears could have imagined. But I wonder if some have chosen to view normal physiological changes that accompany aging as medical problems that require medical solutions.[9]

The author of Ecclesiastes points to a loving, lifelong marital relationship to help us face the challenges of life (9:9). Paul honors singleness as a means of focused service to God, but also offered encouragement to couples for how to honor God and each other by nurturing their ongoing physical relationship (1 Cor. 7).[10] Our sex lives *will* change as we age. Desire may wane. Or both patience and pleasure may increase. One spouse—or both—may face health problems. But each of these sexual changes holds the possibility for continued growth in love.

Growing toward maturity means that our notions of intimacy must extend from what happens in the bedroom to the kind of love authors Margaret Kim Peterson and Dwight Peterson describe here:

> Perhaps what contemporary Christians need is less romance and more love—and we mean real love, not "perfect love." Real love is unitive and community forming; it weaves people together into familial and churchly networks of mutual care and dependence on one another and on God. Husbands and wives, neighbors and friends, children and grandchildren, widows and orphans, all are adopted by God into the household of the church and invited to love and care for one another in ways that certainly include the bond of marriage, but include as well a range of other human relationships—all of which involve real connection, real intimacy, real enjoyment of other people and a real participation in the redemptive work of God in the world.[11]

Becoming sage at menopause means growing in the darkness of Stage 4 faith toward a generative life. As we discover what it is to live in companionship with God, we will seek to reproduce His love in our relationships. We must discover how to embrace a different, deeper kind of beauty as we age.

WHY THAT OLD WOMAN IN MY MIRROR?

Some early morning after you've had four hours of sleep punctuated with random hot flashes, you'll step into the bathroom to brush your teeth and will see a haggard middle-aged woman in your mirror. You'll rub your eyes in hopes of clearing your vision and ask, "Who is this person staring back at me? And what has she done with my younger self?"

At some point in your journey into the second half of your life, you will notice physical changes: a few extra pounds on your abdomen, sagging breasts, a few more gray hairs, and fine lines on your skin that seem to suddenly morph into canyon-sized wrinkles. The late writer Nora Ephron wrote a book about getting older with a title that echoes that sinking feeling we get when we see that middle-aged woman staring us down in the mirror. The book is called *I Feel Bad About My Neck*.

At what age are we most physically attractive? New York dermatologist Gervaise Gerstner told a reporter at the *Wall Street Journal*, "Apparently, 36 is the age that women want to look, based on the photos they bring in."[12] Certainly Hollywood supports this notion, as many older female actors who choose plastic surgery or Botox seem to be aiming at a mythical mid-thirties face. (There are a few notable exceptions to the rule, including Jamie Lee Curtis, Frances McDormand, and Emma Thompson.)

Our culture tells us youth is beauty, and beauty is power. Therapists Vivian Diller and Jill Muir-Sukenick said:

> We anxiously stare into our mirrors like insecure adolescents and are frankly surprised *and* embarrassed that we care so

much. We reject the idea of being solely the object of desire and fantasy, yet who among us does not want to be regarded as attractive? We try seeking comfort from the age-old adage "beauty is in the eye of the beholder," but modern reality tells us *not* to age, that good looks are our currency, our power, and what makes us vital in today's world.[13]

Ask an older woman or man who has been searching for work what they face in the marketplace. The number one response will be age discrimination. Instead of being valued for their experience and wisdom, they're passed over because employers perceive they're too stuck in their ways, too prone to possible health issues, too expensive, too unappealing. In other words, too old. And workplace experts say ageism may begin in some fields as young as 40 for women and 45 for men.[14]

We in the church are not immune from these pressures to look youthful. Popular motivational speaker Joyce Meyer has been open about her facelift;[15] there are other national Christian speakers who don't want to reveal they've sought a doctor's assistance to stay vibrant-looking.[16] But this bias toward youth and beauty can show itself at the local level as well. For instance, worship teams in medium and large-sized churches tend to comprise attractive musicians between the ages of 25–45. A visual is worth a thousand words, and when we in the church appear to give preference to youth and beauty in the same way our culture does, we send the message that those who aren't young or beautiful are less valuable in our community.

On an individual level, however, those who learn to embrace God's continuing transformation of our physical appearance as we age will discover that true beauty has to do with God's work in our lives: "And we all, who with unveiled faces contemplate the Lord's glory, are being transformed into his image with ever-increasing glory, which comes from the Lord, who is the Spirit" (2 Cor. 3:18).

Not long ago, I asked on Facebook at what age my midlife and beyond connections felt most beautiful,[17] I was glad (and a little surprised) to hear that many respondents choose their current life stage. My friend Beth's answer was representative: "I like where I am now, almost 62. For 35+ years my husband has told me every day, 'You're beautiful,' and I finally truly believe it. I have been so much more confident in my 50s and 60s than I was before then. I like who I am and my body doesn't matter so much anymore."

For all the talk we hear in pop culture about accepting ourselves just as we are (while simultaneously trying to match the airbrushed faux perfection of media superstars), I believe that sage believers who feel the same way as Beth does about their looks are living a truly revolutionary message. Maturity is beautiful. It is a message the church and the world need to hear.

FAILING BODIES

Lisa* had been scrupulous about her diet for most of her adult life, avoiding sugar, dairy, gluten, and red meat. She drank plenty of water and exercised regularly. Yet in her fifties, she was diagnosed with an autoimmune disease. Her deteriorating health eventually led to her having to leave a career she loved. She said, "I believe this would have happened earlier in my life if I hadn't been so careful about diet and exercise."

Diet and exercise can make a difference in staving off the effects of aging and illness. But at some point, even the bodies of vegan marathoners begin to stagger under the weight of years—even for those age-defying eighty-five-year-old runners we see online. As we move into maturity, our bodies slow down. Joints need replacing. Cataracts need removal. The Centers for Disease Control lists the top two causes of death for adults ages 45–64 as heart disease and cancer.[18]

Some of us see peers die as we move into midlife; others like Lisa start experiencing health issues that aren't necessarily fatal but require a change in lifestyle to accommodate the limitations of a chronic illness. And just about every one of us discovers that when we catch a cold or spend a crisp autumn afternoon raking leaves in the yard, it seems to take just a little longer to recover than it did when we were younger. (Or a lot longer!)

Our aging, decaying bodies bear witness to our hope of resurrection. However, a sage's resurrection hope doesn't mean we negate the experience of physical suffering by insisting that "a good Christian" remains upbeat and positive at all times. Our faith may give us courage and strength in the face of a terminal cancer diagnosis, but it also means our trust may look like tears. It may mean that our cries of physical or mental anguish will find companionship in the Spirit's intercession for us in His groans too deep for words (Rom. 8:26). There is consolation in knowing even our darkness is not dark to Him (Ps. 139:11–12). Our suffering does not repel Him. In fact, the opposite is true.

Physical and mental deterioration can continue to shape us as people who are held by the love of God until our final breath and beyond:

We know that the one who raised the Lord Jesus from the dead will also raise us with Jesus and present us with you to himself.... Therefore we do not lose heart. Though outwardly we are wasting away, yet inwardly we are being renewed day by day. For our light and momentary troubles are achieving for us an eternal glory that far outweighs them all. So we fix our eyes not on what is seen, but on what is unseen, since what is seen is temporary, but what is unseen is eternal. (2 Cor. 4:14, 16–18)

Becoming sage means growing into the tension of wasting away and being renewed. It is not an either/or proposition, but both/and. As unlovely as the notion of suffering and decay are, Paul tells us here that eternal glory is being created in us through them.

> *Becoming sage means growing into the tension of wasting away and being renewed. It is not an either/or proposition, but both/and.*

Churches that hope to grow in the area of encouraging spiritual formation in the second half of life must do one essential thing: find ways to

show every member of the congregation, no matter what age, how not to lose heart when faced with chronic illness, bodily decay, and the dying process. This can come in the form of practical support for a sick person (meals, house cleaning, driving to appointments) but can also come in the form of large or small group learning (regular input from hospital chaplains and nurses, hospice workers, funeral directors, experts in long-term chronic illness and mental illness).

Our culture tells us our value is tied to youth, attractiveness, sexuality, and health. If we who follow Jesus are growing toward maturity, as we embrace the changes in our bodies, we will become beautifully, radically countercultural as we age.

FOR INDIVIDUAL REFLECTION

1. At what age did you feel most beautiful? Why do you say so? Now, describe your current relationship with your body. When you look in the mirror, what do you see? What frustrates you about your body? What delights you? What does it mean to be "fearfully and wonderfully made" at your present life stage?

2. What are you losing in your life as you enter menopause? What gifts might menopause carry for you? Why?

3. The prophet Isaiah described the Messiah as "a man of suffering, and familiar with pain" (Isa. 53:3). What does this mean to you as you face physical decline and decay? What questions arise in you as you contemplate this truth about Him?

FOR GROUP CONVERSATION

1. Consider this quote from the chapter: "Today in many churches, we hear a low-level form of modern Gnosticism in the way we talk about salvation. When we describe faith in terms of mental assent to facts about God or we equate our ecstatic emotions after a powerful revival service as a measure of His nearness, we feed the erroneous narrative that the spirit is more important than the body. In addition, well-meaning attempts to counteract our culture's approach to sexuality have resulted in messaging in some streams of the church that bodies—in particular, women's bodies—are tempting, dangerous, and bad." Do you see any of this thinking at work in your congregation? If so, why do you think that is?

2. Are people from across the age and wellness spectrum represented on the platform during worship services and in ministry leadership? If not, how can you move beyond the quick fix of token representation (getting older people onto the worship team, for instance) to bring meaningful systemic change to your church culture?

3. First Corinthians 6:19–20 tells us that God values our bodies so much that He places His Spirit within believers: "Do you not know that your bodies are temples of the Holy Spirit, who is in you, whom you have received from God? You are not your own; you were bought at a price. Therefore honor God with your bodies." How does your church community respond to this imperative? Are there ways in which you could improve?

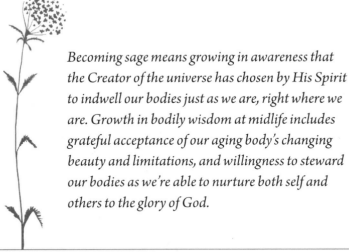

Becoming sage means growing in awareness that the Creator of the universe has chosen by His Spirit to indwell our bodies just as we are, right where we are. Growth in bodily wisdom at midlife includes grateful acceptance of our aging body's changing beauty and limitations, and willingness to steward our bodies as we're able to nurture both self and others to the glory of God.

CHAPTER 7

YOU CAN'T TAKE IT WITH YOU

Financial discipleship beyond formulas

During the 1980s, folksy financial advisor Larry Burkett taught Christians how to manage their money. A generation later, Dave Ramsey's Financial Peace University brought similar conservative money management principles to the next generation in the church. A few of the common sense tenets taught by these conservative experts included:

- Build a personal emergency fund.
- Pay off credit cards.
- Avoid consumer debt.
- Buy an affordable home and make it your priority to prepay on that mortgage.
- Save for big purchases, children's higher education, and retirement.

- Tithe 10 percent of your income to your church and seek to give generously above that amount to other ministries and causes you care about.

Thousands, including my husband and me, have been helped by this kind of sensible financial counsel. I believe at least a few of us understood that if these programs were endorsed by our local churches, they carried with them an implicit promise that God would protect and bless our money if only we followed the plan.

As we become sage, we'll find ourselves reassessing every aspect of our life and faith practice in order to move beyond following principles toward creating meaning. This includes our finances. Christian philosopher and sociologist Jacques Ellul pointed out that when Jesus called money "mammon" in Matthew 6:24 and Luke 16:13 (KJV), he wasn't using a common reference drawn from the culture around Him. Though we tend to think that we are the ones who ascribe value and power to money, by personifying the notion of wealth with the name "mammon," Jesus was saying the opposite is true. He told His hearers that money has a specific moral and spiritual power in this world that demands our allegiance and shapes our priorities.[1] Both God and mammon ask of us who we will serve. We simply can't answer "both."

In recent decades, some in the church have tried to tell us that serving both is possible. Though many of us may eschew the most egregious forms of "prosperity preaching," the notion that God will bless us with health and wealth if we give or serve sacrificially, milder forms of it are at work among us. Writer Brandon Peach said:

The pursuit of middle-class comfort is, if not uniquely American, woven into the fabric of the American Dream. As Christians, we often fall into the assumption or belief that God desires very much that we be comfortable, when throughout Scripture, this idea is challenged again and again. The "prosperity gospel" would have us believe that God wants us all to be wealthy, self-sufficient, cozy.

Its analog in the wider Church isn't necessarily that God wants us to be rich, but perhaps a little bit richer. A little bit more successful. A little bit better off.[2]

Many analysts believe the financial crisis of 2007–2008 was the most serious since the Great Depression in the 1930s.[3] Like most Americans up to that point, my husband and I viewed home ownership as a secure investment. We weren't prepared for the impact of seeing our home decrease in value by nearly 70 percent by early 2012. We joined the ranks of ten million homeowners during that period who ended up losing their homes via foreclosure or short sale.[4]

At one point during our short sale process, we met with a local financial advisor for guidance. During the discussion, he asked my husband and me to name our financial fears no matter how big or small they were. Mine ranged from "We won't have enough money for our retirement" and "We'll be homeless" all the way to "I won't be able to buy a cute new pair of shoes if I need ... or (*ahem*) want ... them."

Up to that point, I thought I had "solved" the problem of mammon's power in my life by trying to adhere to a formula. However, naming my fears as we were poised to lose both money and shelter revealed to me that I had a lot to learn.

Spiritual growth in the area of our financial resources means moving beyond the kind of reliance on sure-fire formulas that seemed to serve us during earlier stages of our faith formation. In 2012, I discovered that I'd relied on what Brandon Peach described as a Christianized version of the American Dream to set my expectations and guide my life.

The American Dream has formed most of us more than we realize. American-born missionary Amy Medina discovered that she carried deeply-held assumptions about what constitutes a God-blessed life, even after nearly two decades in Tanzania. She realized that economic security, comfort, and cultural homogeneity shaped her ideals, and she did some powerful reflecting on what this meant to her faith, writing on her blog,

> Why do I assume that He owes me a peaceful American dream-life, when He doesn't grant it to almost any other Christian anywhere in the world? . . .
>
> . . . God does not owe American Christians anything. He does not owe me a savings account or health insurance. He does not guarantee that my children will have the opportunity to go to college and become prosperous citizens. He does not promise religious freedom, or pleasant vacations, or safety on American streets. He doesn't even promise that America will continue to exist as we know it.[5]

Medina's sobering words are meant to help us untangle the hold our culture's values have on our faith.

Money questions may be what God uses to bring you to the limits of faith Stages 1, 2, and 3. You may find yourself in the darkness of Stage 4 whether a financial crisis hastens your journey there, or you find yourself there as you begin to reckon more intimately about what the rest of your life may look like. Scripture coaches us to use diligence in preparing for the future (Gen. 41:48–49; Prov. 6:6–11) while coaxing us to hold those plans loosely (Prov. 27:1; James 4:15). A sage learns to live in the tension between those two directives. At the same time, as we grow, we will move from building our lives during the first half of our adulthood into seeking to make meaning during the second half. That quest can't adequately be answered with the American Dream.

Jesus underscored throughout His ministry that God's "economy" was not like that of the world (Luke 10:25–37).

He affirmed what the Law had to say about giving, while at the same time calling for His followers to move beyond thinking in terms of rules to focusing on sacrificial living (Mark 10:17–27; Luke 16:19–31). He taught us to combat mammon's hold on our souls by recognizing it is a tool and not a master (Luke 16:1–9), focusing on eternity here and now (Matt. 6:19–21; Luke 12:16–21), and commending generosity to the poor and marginalized (Matt. 25:31–46; Luke 10:25–37). He reminded us we are not exempt from our responsibility to be a "good neighbor" to our families (Matt. 19:19) and as participants in our culture (Mark 12:17).

And He reminded us in the hours before His death that God is looking for a wholehearted response from each one of us, no matter what our socioeconomic status is:

> Jesus sat down opposite the place where the offerings were put and watched the crowd putting their money into the temple treasury. Many rich people threw in large amounts. But a poor widow came and put in two very small copper coins, worth only a few cents.

Calling his disciples to him, Jesus said, "Truly I tell you, this poor widow has put more into the treasury than all the others. They all gave out of their wealth; but she, out of her poverty, put in everything—all she had to live on." (Mark 12:41–44)[6]

In the Ancient Near East, widowhood was a classification signaling the bottom of the economic and social ladder.[7] Just as He'd done throughout His ministry, Jesus upended the standard social strata when He took note of this unnamed widow. Her two coins wouldn't be enough to purchase half of a Happy Meal today. She wasn't giving because she was checking off the boxes on a sure-fire financial plan. Instead, her suffering and loss led her to a whole-life response of surrender and gratitude to the God she loved. Her example leaves us a priceless legacy.

PASS IT ON

"Legacy" can be a loaded word when it comes to money. Estate planners and charities use the word to help potential benefactors connect with the idea that bequeathing money and property to heirs is meant to be more than just a financial transaction.

Stories like Sylvia Bloom's underscore this reality. Bloom was a widow living in a modest one-bedroom apartment in Brooklyn. She worked as a secretary at a Manhattan law firm until she was 96 years old. When she died the following year, people were stunned to discover she'd left behind a fortune. She left six million dollars to a New York City social services organization and another two million to various scholarship funds.

In her profile of secret millionaire donors like Bloom, writer Juliana LaBianca said, "These unassuming philanthropists share some qualities. The most obvious is that they often have no children. That's one reason many of them were able to save so much of their humble paychecks. It also means they had no direct natural heirs." She noted that people like Bloom thought long and hard about how their supersized savings might make a difference in the lives of others. In other words, their legacy.[8]

A legacy can be financial, and it can also be something less tangible that is passed down from an earlier generation, such as being a fourth-gen master baker. As Christians, we commit to pass on a legacy of faith to our children and grandchildren, per Deuteronomy 6:4–9. We hear this commitment amplified in language like this:

- We will not hide them from their descendants; we will tell the next generation the praiseworthy deeds of the LORD, his power, and the wonders he has done. (Ps. 78:4)
- One generation commends your works to another; they tell of your mighty acts. (Ps. 145:4)
- I have no greater joy than to hear that my children are walking in the truth. (3 John 4)

We may die penniless, but in passing on our faith, we offer our children and their children an eternal inheritance. We also bequeath to our families physical, non-monetary things (ranging from our DNA to, perhaps, those baking skills) that we've received from our forebears. When we're contemplating the role money has in passing on a legacy, we must frame it in terms of the bigger picture of everything we're hoping to pass down.

Proverbs 13:22 says, "A good person leaves an inheritance for their children's children, but a sinner's wealth is stored up for the righteous." This passage speaks to far more than the material goods we'll leave behind. The word for inheritance in this verse, *nachal,* is a verb that carries the connotation of heritage. In other words, good people create a legacy of good character. And those who've made their fortune from sleazy dealings have nothing of lasting value to pass on to their heirs.

If we're growing toward maturity, we will also grow in our desire to create a meaningful legacy.

If we're growing toward maturity, we will also grow in our desire to create a meaningful legacy. The quest to make meaning of our lives may mean some of us will choose to use our financial resources to begin a new business, return to school to change careers, or pour ourselves in new ways into ministry or service. This desire may shrink a future inheritance dollar amount to our children but may leave behind a far more lasting legacy.

Increasingly, our kids don't want our cherished family heirlooms. Millennials (born 1981–1996) and Gen Z children (born 1996 to the present) are eschewing antique teacup collections and dining room sets that we've been warehousing for them in our homes. Do an online search for "Kids don't want their parents' stuff" and you'll be rewarded with thousands of articles discussing this trend. Some of the reasons for this generational shift include changing tastes, a desire for experience over accumulation of material goods, and delayed marriage and non-permanent living arrangements.[9] Our earthly treasures may not have as much value to our children as they've had to us.

Whether our wills list our children, friends, extended family, or cherished ministries as beneficiaries once we're gone, we are creating our true legacy each day of our lives before we're gone.

FEARING THE FUTURE

As I learned when I listed my anxieties with our financial advisor, money questions plus an uncertain future often equals fear. Will we have enough to carry us to the end of our days once we can no longer work full-time?

There is no sure-fire, economy impervious financial plan that will shelter and provide for my family and me. My husband and I must continue to work and plan carefully for the future, leaning deeply into God's wisdom about the legacy He is asking us to create. And we must do so repudiating the lies mammon hisses at us: that God will not shelter or provide for us. As we confront those lies and the fear they engender in us with God's truth, we will learn as apprentices the lessons we need to learn at every life stage: nothing can separate us from the love of Christ (Rom. 8:31–39).

Spiritual formation in the area of our finances at midlife is another facet of the call to discipleship. Most of us have more to lose at this point of our lives. As He has each step of our journey, Jesus asks us to release our grip on the things we are clutching in hopes of securing our future so we are free to follow Him—even when we know following Him will lead us toward the end of our lives on earth:

"Whoever wants to be my disciple must deny themselves and take up their cross and follow me. For whoever wants to save their life will lose it, but whoever loses their life for me and for the gospel will save it. What good is it for someone to gain the whole world, yet forfeit their soul? Or what can anyone give in exchange for their soul?" (Mark 8:34–37)

Many of us hear first in these words a call to heroic following of the kind we celebrate among martyrs and missionaries. However, at midlife and beyond, we grow evermore aware we are journeying toward death. Money can't save us from this end. But there is good news. To pick up the cross is to surrender to Jesus on this journey and discover the riches of His salvation. Our true legacy is formed foremost from our sage character.

FOR INDIVIDUAL REFLECTION

1. Reread missionary Amy Medina's words about God not owing American Christians anything. What questions arise in you as you consider her observations?

2. Have you faced a significant financial challenge or setback? What was the experience like for you? What did you discover about yourself? About God?

3. Use your imagination to write an obituary for the poor widow described in Mark 12:41–44. How would you describe her legacy? Ask God in prayer to guide you as you consider the legacy you are creating in your life.

FOR GROUP CONVERSATION

1. What are the strengths and limitations of the American Dream? How has the American Dream shaped your church culture?

2. How does your church talk about money?

3. Think beyond your congregation's mission or vision statements. Reflect on the history of your church—including the difficult stuff: splits, controversies, sins, and the stories of those who've left as a result of these things. Consider the lives that have been changed and strengthened, both within your church and as a result of ministry efforts in your community and beyond. What kind of legacy is your congregation creating?

Becoming sage moves toward a commitment to create a legacy. That legacy may include our money and possessions, but year by year, as we move toward death, we recognize that our legacy is not created primarily with our stuff but by our character.

CHAPTER 8

HAPPINESS IS
SPELLED WITH A "U"

*The essential task of nurturing emotional
and spiritual health*

Did you know that happiness is spelled with a "u"?

A 2017 *Washington Post* piece highlighted an analysis of life satisfaction surveys that number-crunched data from 1.3 million respondents in more than fifty countries. Writer Christopher Ingraham said:

> Happiness, those surveys show, follow a generalized U-shape over the course of a life: People report high degrees of happiness in their late teens and early 20s. But as the years roll by, people become more and more miserable, hitting a nadir in life satisfaction sometime around the early 50s. Happiness rebounds from there into old age and retirement.[1]

Author Barbara Bradley Haggerty highlighted the work done by researcher Andrew Oswald around this U-shaped happiness curve, noting:

> Whether in the United States or Saudi Arabia, Zimbabwe or Moldova, happiness dips in the forties. Oswald said that you cannot blame middle-aged misery on circumstances, since the researchers controlled for factors such as unemployment, health problems, and divorce. Rather, he said, it is something "deep inside" that causes the malaise, almost as if we're "wired for misery."[2]

Just because this misery is common doesn't mean it's not serious. The Centers for Disease Control and Prevention noted that while overall suicide rates have climbed significantly in recent years, those ages 45 to 64 comprise the highest proportion of this number. In fact, there has been an alarming 45 percent increase in suicides among this age group over the last seventeen years.[3]

In some streams of the church, people sliding to the bottom of the U have picked up unhelpful messaging, either denying that this kind of depression exists in the life of a growing Christian or suggesting that these feelings are sinful and can be vanquished by aggressive application of Scripture. For every person who has found a measure of solace in denial or in choosing to treat emotional misery as sin, I suspect many others like my friend Kim find those options both isolating and unhelpful.

Kim* kept trying to pep talk herself out of that sense of despair that saturated her days like a gray fog. "I have a busy, great life," she told me. "My husband and I have financial security, our kids have launched from the nest without the same kind of drama some of my friends are experiencing, and we're in good health. My real estate career is going well. I'm leading a women's Bible study at church. I just got asked to join the board of a non-profit serving my community . . ." Her voice trailed off. "I don't know what's wrong with me. I'm weary of it all. To make matters worse, I can't seem to make myself care anymore." She assured me she wasn't suicidal but couldn't seem to shake the thick fog that shrouded her life, a life she felt should have been marked by joy. Her shame at not being able to claim that joy continued to keep her swirling slowly around the bottom of that U-curve as if she was circling a drain.

As we discussed in chapter 2, we may find ourselves feeling as through we're groping in the darkness as we hit the metaphorical wall of Stage 4 faith. That darkness may be amplified by the emotional landscape of the U-curve.

Was Kim experiencing midlife malaise? Clinical depression? Or what the ancients used to call *acedia*, or spiritual apathy?

BEYOND THE BLUES

Where does midlife malaise end and depression begin? Writers from the National Institute for Mental Health offers this checklist of symptoms for depression:

- Persistent sad, anxious, or "empty" mood
- Feelings of hopelessness or pessimism
- Irritability
- Feelings of guilt, worthlessness, or helplessness
- Loss of interest or pleasure in hobbies and activities

- Decreased energy or fatigue
- Moving or talking more slowly
- Feeling restless or having trouble sitting still
- Difficulty concentrating, remembering, or making decisions
- Difficulty sleeping, early-morning awakening, or oversleeping
- Appetite and/or weight changes
- Thoughts of death or suicide, or suicide attempts
- Aches or pains, headaches, cramps, or digestive problems without a clear physical cause and/or that do not ease even with treatment[4]

They note that if you've had some of these symptoms for at least two weeks, it may be depression. In addition, they add the following clarifying words about this list:

Not everyone who is depressed experiences every symptom. Some people experience only a few symptoms while others may experience many. Several persistent symptoms in addition to low mood are required for a diagnosis of major depression, but people with only a few—but distressing— symptoms may benefit from treatment of their "subsyndromal" depression.[5]

Some illnesses, including cancer, diabetes, and heart disease, can contribute to depression, and a number of prescription medications can exacerbate depression symptoms, especially for those at midlife and beyond. Though it's often called "the common cold" of mental illness, the metaphor breaks down because depression isn't contagious.[6] Its frequency, however, exacts a high cost from our culture. One recent study noted that for every dollar spent treating depression, we spend more than six dollars on related illnesses, reduced workplace productivity, and the losses associated with suicide.[7]

I have been heartened to see the way in which the church has begun to play a role in de-stigmatizing mental illness. The advocacy efforts of leaders like Kay Warren and Amy Simpson and the commitment of the National Alliance for Mental Illness (NAMI) to partner with faith-based organizations in a community through their FaithNet initiative are a welcome change in direction.[8] But the stigma still exists in some pockets of the church. Too many of us have seen mental illness treated as though it were a sin, which can make it even harder than it already is to seek help when it hits close to home.

I was smack-dab in prime U-curve territory when I realized that I wasn't dealing with midlife malaise, but a serious case of clinical depression. For several months running, I could check off every single bullet point on the National Institute for Mental Health list. The one on the list that got me to pick up the phone and find a licensed professional counselor was the fact that I'd begun praying my life would simply come to an end, not because I ached to be with the Lord in the way the apostle Paul had expressed in 2 Corinthians 5:6–8, but because there was no end in sight to the darkness. I'd had blue periods earlier in my life, but none persisted like this one had.

Thanks be to God, I was able to find an excellent licensed counselor. Though I would not have been opposed to medication to help stabilize my mood, my counselor determined that talk therapy, focused on working through the series of significant

Some who seek counseling and/or medication may deal with a misplaced sense of shame or discomfort about needing help.

losses I'd experienced, would be most helpful for me. My darkness didn't dissipate all at once, but one day, I noticed that food had begun tasting good again, and another day, I realized getting out of bed each morning no longer depleted every drop of energy I had.

In general, some who seek counseling and/or medication may deal with a misplaced sense of shame or discomfort about needing help. I believe this shame or discomfort may be exacerbated among many Christians because we function with the idea that our faith should be able to triumph over all the effects and limitations of our human condition. This kind of thinking places a burden on us we were never meant to bear.

Jesus ministered to those who expressed faith in Him (Matt. 15:21–28) and cared for those who weren't able to reach out to Him (Luke 8:26–39). He used a variety of means to bring kingdom restoration to those who needed healing. He still does. For some of us battling depression or other forms of mental illness, He may choose to use physicians and counselors. The only one who ultimately benefits from isolating us, shaming us, and keeping us from reaching out to get the help we need is Satan, the enemy of our souls (John 10:10; 1 Peter 5:8).

Not all of us who find ourselves experiencing the gravity of the U-curve will become clinically depressed. But those who do may find the climb upward from that seemingly endless bottom is made easier with some help. And the humility and honesty of seeking medical or counseling help when it's necessary may be key to your journey through the dark night of Stage 4 faith.

WEARY SOULS

Not all depression is physiological in nature. There is also a form of spiritual depression early church fathers and mothers called *acedia*, a word rooted in the Greek that means "absence of care." Writing in the thirteenth century, Thomas Aquinas described it as "a certain oppressive sadness, which so depresses man's mind that he can do nothing freely . . . a certain weariness in working . . . a torpor of the mind that neglects to begin good things."[9] Eventually, this definition was shorthanded to refer to the sin of sloth, but that single word doesn't capture the restlessness and disconnection that can be a part of acedia.

Author Kathleen Norris's 2008 memoir *Acedia and Me* offers a fuller explanation:

> I believe that such standard dictionary definitions of *acedia* as "apathy," "boredom," or "torpor" do not begin to cover it, and while we may find it convenient to regard it as a more primitive word for what we now term depression, the truth is more complex. . . .
>
> Acedia, it seems, is not only the demon that lobs an assault at midday but also the bad thought that afflicts us in the middle of life, when it seems impossible to care about so many things that used to matter. . . . The pose of indifference is far more appealing.[10]

Norris notes that "while depression is an illness treatable by counseling and medication, acedia is a vice that is best countered by spiritual practice and the discipline of prayer."[11]

After a thorough checkup by her physician to rule out any physiological factors, my friend Kim spent a bit of time with a counselor who focused on helping her prioritize some of her commitments. She dropped a few activities, which gave her busy-busy schedule some margin. But it took some honest conversations and prayer with a mature-in-the-Lord friend for Kim to discern that the root of her problem wasn't primarily emotional in nature but spiritual. Her feelings of boredom and restlessness seemed rooted in a relationship with God that had become lifeless and task-oriented.

However, this realization didn't flip a switch that instantly revived her soul. She discovered that acedia has a gravity all its own, which seemed to want to anchor her in the U-curve in which she found herself at midlife.

The language of "spiritual warfare" has been hyper-dramatized by some popular works of Christian fiction or has led some streams of the church to focus in unhealthy ways on cosmic conflict as the cause of every personal struggle we might face. Satan's designs on our lives rarely look like the high drama of superhero movies. In addition, it is poor theology to understand ourselves as helpless pawns trapped in a battle between two equal forces, God and Satan.[12] This error results in believers vastly underestimating the power of God—who has no equal.[13]

While some forms of spiritual warfare can be very dramatic, our battleground can be as subtle as the world-weariness of acedia. The description of the armor of God in Ephesians 6:11–17 is a reminder that we must choose to don a variety of defensive and offensive tools in order to resist the schemes of the enemy of our souls. But even when we can't—if we're held in the grip of conditions like mental illness or acedia, for example—we can rest in the reality that the Lord fights for us (Ex. 14:14; 2 Thess. 3:3). Perhaps all we may be able to pray is, "I can't do it. Please help me."

Jesus knows our weakness and stands for us when we buckle under the weight of our own brokenness. The writer of Hebrews offers assurance: "For we do not have a high priest who is unable to empathize with our weaknesses, but we have one who has been tempted in every way, just as we are—yet he did not sin" (Heb. 4:15).

Combatting acedia calls for a unique-to-you combination of both resting in the finished work of Christ on your behalf and exercising a bit of discipline to combat your spiritual inertia. Like so many other realities of midlife, there is no program or quick fix. Sometimes simple rest is the best medicine, especially if acedia follows years of Stage 3 faith that results in laboring to the point of burnout for Jesus. Asking God to search our hearts and reveal places where sin has taken root is an essential spiritual discipline in every stage of our lives, and in cases where acedia may be at play, regularly praying this question can nudge us forward even when we feel spiritually stuck. In yet other circumstances, a bit of energy applied in the form of continuing to serve, pray, study, and worship God, even if the rewards aren't instant, may eventually lead to renewal.

If you're feeling as though you're idling in neutral, I commend the practice of seeking out a mature, faithful friend with whom you can be honest, or consider seeking out the companionship and counsel of a trained spiritual director to support, challenge, and pray with you.

Stages 2 ("God, I belong to you") and 3 ("God, I'm working for you") of our journeys of faith can contain a good measure of hubris and a heaping helping of self-certain pride. It is a confidence building thing to feel as if you belong to something—or Someone—much bigger than yourself and that what you're doing matters for all eternity. The U-curve, along with the related challenges some face of either mental illness and/or acedia at midlife, underscores the process by which hubris can become humility as we learn to follow God through the darkness of Stage 4 growth.

SAGE EMOTIONS

Loving God heart, soul, mind, and strength means that we will be moving toward emotional maturity just as we are moving toward physical, intellectual, and spiritual maturity.

Pastor Pete Scazzero was the leader of a rapidly growing congregation in Queens, New York, when his wife, Geri, told him she no longer wanted to attend his church. He may have been an "effective" church leader, but the stress and toxic emotional life he was living at home had depleted Geri. She told Pete she no longer respected his ability to pastor her.

The confrontation brought many other issues to a head in Scazzero's life. He may have been an "effective" leader, but he wasn't a healthy, loving one. It turned out that Geri wasn't the only one who'd been wounded by him. His crisis led him to get counseling and to seek spiritual direction. As a result, he began to do the hard work of excavating the "why" that simmered just under the surface of his take-no-prisoners approach to ministry and life.

Scazzero contends that emotional maturity is not disconnected from spiritual maturity, citing markers of emotional health that mirror that of spiritual vigor—things like recognizing and managing our own feelings and practicing appropriate expressions of sexuality. Scazzero says that while a person can grow in these areas without Christ, coupling a commitment to emotional health with pursuit of a deeper life with Him is where meaningful transformation occurs. This deeper life can involve surrender to God in every situation and discovering healthy rhythms with God that aren't based on our to-do lists, among many other things.[14]

God is at work through our emotions—yes, including those in the bottom of the U-curve, those that accompany mental health challenges, and those that flow out of a disordered spiritual life—to move us toward a sage expression of faith.

FOR INDIVIDUAL REFLECTION

1. If you are at midlife or beyond, have you noticed the U-curve at play in your life? In the lives of others you know? If so, how?

2. Reflect on the armor of God detailed in Ephesians 6:11–17. Though it is likely you've never physically worn the kind of armor referenced in the passage, take a few minutes to consider what truths this passage holds about the way in which you can fight the spiritual battles you're currently facing. The virtues named in these verses reflect some essential aspects of God's character. Recognize that your battles hold an invitation to know God better.

3. Review the discussion of acedia in this chapter. What practices would you commend to someone you know who may be battling this condition? What might you tell them to avoid?

FOR GROUP CONVERSATION

1. How do the leaders of your congregation speak of mental illness? What resources and support do you have to offer those who are dealing with mental illness themselves and/or in their families?

2. Have you identified mature, discerning, safe sages in your congregation who can walk alongside those at midlife who may find themselves battling the effects of the U-curve? Do you have names of trusted spiritual directors who can provide more specific care and direction for those who are struggling with acedia? If not, is this something that seems of value to you in your church context? Why or why not?

3. Author Pete Scazzero said, "It's impossible to be spiritually mature while remaining emotionally immature."[15] How have you seen this play out in a former or present church setting?

Becoming sage means embracing the entire range of our own human emotion as Jesus does and seeking the discernment of trusted friends, advocates, and counselors when necessary.

CHAPTER 9

FROM DOING TO BEING

*Vocation is much more than
what's on a resume*

I never imagined my five high school BFFs and I were a clique. We were bound to one another by the excitement of our newfound faith in Jesus and tried hard to invite others to know Him too, which meant that the boundaries of our social circle were fairly porous. But we also played an outsized role in one another's lives as we faced those first big decisions about who each one of us was going to be as we moved beyond high school. Nowhere was our cliquishness more evident than when we each had to make decisions during senior year about where to attend college and what major to choose.

Because our high school was the magnet school for all the deaf students in the northwest suburbs of Chicago, we'd always had sign language interpreters in our classrooms, and our school offered courses in sign for interested hearing students. The opportunity to learn to communicate so we could befriend the deaf students drew most of us to study sign in my "we're-not-a-clique" group.

Each one of us was animated by a God-given desire to make a difference by serving others, which mixed with the missionary zeal of our newfound faith and our unhealthy reliance on one another as a sort of surrogate family. When it came time to choose a college and major, all six of us felt led to attend Illinois State University and to major in special education or a closely related field.

It's hard to believe that no one in our lives seemed to question this seemingly miraculous congruence of callings, but I doubt any of us would have listened anyway. My high school friends shared with me the joy of falling in love with Jesus. In some ways, we all fell in love with Him together, and our bond was very, very deep.

God knew we served as one another's training wheels as each of us rolled toward adulthood, and He graciously permitted all six of us to begin college in Normal, Illinois. Of the six, two graduated four years later with degrees in special education. One has been in the field for over thirty years and has earned a doctorate along the way. Another led a classroom of deaf students for several years before moving to a mainstream elementary school classroom, where she continues to teach. A third received a degree in recreational therapy and worked in that field for decades. The three of them found career paths that were a good fit for them.

The other three, including me, never completed our undergraduate degrees. Though my high school pals have maintained some level of connection with one another through the years, our paths diverged as each of us moved into young adulthood. One of the first lessons we all had to learn was that there was no one-size-fits-six answer to the questions each one of us faced about how to build an adult life.

None of us had begun to explore an even more essential question than that of career choice—the question of vocation. Most use the words "career" and "vocation" interchangeably, conflated to mean "an occupation, preferably with opportunities for growth." This may be true of career, but the word "vocation" literally means "calling." As a teen, I knew I wanted a career that would help others. But I had no idea how to begin thinking more deeply about why I'd been created and what God had called me to bring to the world.

At least, not then.

After I dropped out of college at the end of my sophomore year, the future loomed before me like the Grand Canyon. I felt I had to come up with a Plan B, stat! If I wasn't going to be a teacher, what could I do? I looked at myself in the funhouse mirror of other people's lives and used those inaccurate reflections of myself as clues that would help me discern a career path.

For instance, I had a friend who was a bank teller. I decided if banking was a good career for him, it was obvious that it would be a good career for me, too. I was so poorly suited for the job that when the person training me told me that it didn't seem like I was catching on and would need to take the unusual step of going through at least another week of "remedial" training, I told her that I didn't think forty years of training would turn me into a good bank teller. I thanked her for her time, apologized for wasting it, and resigned.

I looked at myself through the mirrors held up by the people at my new church too. There I learned the highest form of Christian service was to be a missionary in a foreign land. For a while, I entertained this as a career possibility because I wanted to do Big Things for God, and there didn't seem to be any bigger thing than getting off a plane in a foreign country and telling people about Jesus. It took me a long time to admit that my zeal to become a missionary had more to do with being able to answer people's questions about what I was planning to do with my life after I dropped out of college than any sort of deep care for people living in a distant place who didn't know Jesus.

MIRROR, MIRROR

Looking into the mirrors held up by others to discern life direction is a hallmark of young adulthood, according to educator Parker Palmer. When he was a young man in the 1960s, he took his life cues from reformers like Dorothy Day and Martin Luther King:

> So I lined up the loftiest ideals I could find and set out to achieve them. The results were rarely admirable, often laughable, and sometimes grotesque. But always they were unreal, a distortion of my true self—as must be the case when one lives from the outside in, not the inside out. I had simply found a "noble" way to live a life that was not my own, a life spent imitating heroes instead of listening to my heart.[1]

Some of us try to live up to the aspirations our parents or other significant influencers have for us. Some imitate the lives of others we admire, as Palmer did, hoping to build a life that looks like theirs. And for reasons ranging from healthy individuation to angry rebellion, others choose a path diametrically opposed to the values or dreams their parents had for them, which is an upside-down way to respond to what they think they see in their mirror.

God wired within human beings the responsibility to exercise dominion over creation (Gen. 1:28). We see this good design at work from the time we're very young, learning to share our toys and help with household chores. This need to exercise dominion is evidenced in the ambitions and life-building choices of young adulthood.

I saw a variation of my own "call to the mission field" career path among some young men and women I got to know when I worked at a seminary. They'd learned to cloak their ambitions in Christian-y language about calling and service, but I'd heard variations of the same theme from several through the years: "I'll be a youth pastor after graduation so I can get my foot in the door of a church job. Then I can work my way up to senior pastor. I'm called to *preach*."

Certainly, aspiration is not limited to seminarians. A world-class chef starts out as a dishwasher in a restaurant, his dreams of more propelling him past the entry-level grunt work. A stay-at-home mom may funnel her ambition into being the best mother ever, driven to make every day Instagram perfect. A bank president often begins as a teller, which is why I'll never be a bank president.

It still bothers me that those ambitious seminary students viewed youth ministry as a way to pay their dues as they climbed the ladder of career success, all in the name of serving God. I

believed many of the kids to whom they were ministering probably smelled those mixed motives. And sadly, as those same youth
pastors project their own drives onto young teens, telling them
God is calling every single one of them to be world-changers,
they may be lighting a rocket under another generation who may
eventually discover that a measure of their zeal and big dreams
came from the mirror of their youth pastor.

TIME TO DISMANTLE

The author of Ecclesiastes observed that there are seasons (literally, "appointed times") in each chapter of our lives. There is
"a time to tear down and a time to build" (Eccl. 3:3). Midlife is
the season when what we've built during the first half of our lives
is often downsized, reordered, or dismantled entirely. Spiritual
growth at midlife means that we begin to recognize the mirrors
we've used to define our identity don't accurately reflect who we
truly are.

In their book *The Critical Journey*, authors Janet Hagberg and
Robert Guelich note that our sense of who we are is challenged
by the losses and changes that come naturally during this season
of our lives:

> We didn't think we'd be invited to suffer. [Life] doesn't seem
> to be moving in the direction we'd assumed it would. That
> alone is a good clue that we are still on the journey at this
> stage—when the obvious is not in the plan. Once again we are
> asked to suspend our judgment, to trust even more deeply in
> our new relationship with God, and to continue the work of
> surrender as part of the transformation process.[2]

That surrender rarely comes in an instant. But as God prunes and reshapes us as we enter midlife, He uses those losses to help us find our way to a sage expression of the vocation with which He's gifted us.

This is illustrated beautifully in Naomi's story found in the book of Ruth. In the first chapter, we meet Naomi at midlife as we are parachuted into her story after her husband and two sons died. She'd always poured herself into her family, which is a high calling and the essential description of her life to that point. Her commitment to her family showed itself in the deep affection her sons' wives Orpah and Ruth had with her. Though they were from a different culture and people group than she was, Naomi helped them to know the God she served, though she was living far from her own home.

The three widows could not survive in that culture on their own. Naomi tried to send the young women back to their families to find help, and she set her sights on the long desert journey back to her own home town of Bethlehem. Her daughters-in-law clinged to her, begging not to be separated from her. Eventually Naomi convinced Orpah to leave, but Ruth refused. She did not wish to leave Naomi's side—or her God.

It is in the midst of this emotional exchange with the two young women that we discover Naomi's new understanding of herself: "'Don't call me Naomi,' she told them. 'Call me Mara, because the Almighty has made my life very bitter. I went away full, but the LORD has brought me back empty. Why call me Naomi? The LORD has afflicted me; the Almighty has brought misfortune upon me'" (Ruth 1:20–21).

Naomi means my delight; Mara means bitter. Naomi's life

had been pruned to the bone.

As we read Naomi's story through the remaining three chapters of the book of Ruth, we see that despite her despair, Naomi exercises her faith, knowledge, and wisdom to build a new life for herself and Ruth out of the losses of her old life. Naomi understood how to communicate with clarity with the men in her world, how to mentor her daughter-in-law, and how to live faithfully with the deep grief she'd carry with her the rest of her days. The end of the book presents a vivid picture of Naomi cradling Ruth's newborn son in her arms (Ruth 4:16). This son would become the grandfather of King David, part of the lineage of the Messiah Jesus (Matt. 1:5–6). She proclaims to us the way in which loss can bring forth a true sense of vocation.

GOD SPEAKS THROUGH TEARS

Author Frederick Buechner said,

> Whenever you find tears in your eyes, especially unexpected tears, it is well to pay the closest attention. They are not only telling you something about the secret of who you are but, more often than not, God is speaking to you through them of the mystery of where you have come from and is summoning you to where, if your soul is to be saved, you should go to next.[3]

What moves you? What brings you to tears?

You will never see these questions on a high school career aptitude test, and I daresay few of us would be able to answer it fully at that point of our lives amidst the cacophony of mirrors and ambitions. Whether they are physical tears or simply the cries of your heart, your tears may flow from your compassion, fear, anger, joy, loneliness, or grief—or, more likely, some unique-to-you combination of the above.

They all matter, even the tears that may at first appear to you to be selfish or sinful. Stay with them. Ask questions of those tears. If you feel you are swimming in a pool of self-pity because of a job loss, for example, please bring the sin in that to Jesus. But also bring your sorrow to Him and ask Him to guide you as you begin to come to terms with what you've lost as a result of that pink slip.

Relationships? Financial security? Aggravation at bad workplace politics? A sense of purpose?

If midlife finds you soul-weary and short of tears, I commend to you the words of the founder of World Vision, Bob Pierce, who said, "Let my heart be broken by the things that break the heart of God."

Our fully human, fully divine Savior wept over the untimely death of His beloved friend Lazarus, His tears mingling with those who were sorrowing over his passing (John 11:35). He wept tears of brokenhearted anger over the way in which worship of His Father had been distorted by selfish human "religious" activity (Luke 19:41–44). And His cries of pain, anguish, and sorrow from the cross were tears of suffering, desolation, and perfect love (Matt. 27:45–50).

Like many of her age peers, Janice* was drawn to political activism when she was young, but eventually channeled her countercultural fire into being among the first generation of homeschool parents. Her birth children were teens, well on their way toward launching into adulthood, when she began asking deeper questions about who God was calling her to be in the next act of her life. She was drawn to stories and images of children languishing in foster care. She began offering temporary shelter in her home for babies in need of short-term care.

Janice knew she couldn't change the world but believed, along with her husband, that they could change the world for an older child or two waiting for a forever home. This was the spot where the tears flowed for her. The pair immersed themselves in learning about the effects of a birth parent's drug addiction on a baby, about trauma, abandonment, learning disabilities, abuse, and the far-reaching effects of reactive attachment disorder. The challenges energized both of them, and before they knew it, their emptying nest had been filled to overflowing with two special needs siblings who'd been in the foster care system for years. Her youthful passion to change the world led her in unexpected ways to discover her true vocation: to nurture those who'd been deeply damaged by their families of origin.

Not all those asking questions about vocation in the second half of life take on a dramatic new life assignment as Janice did. Instead, it may mean scaling way back. In her early fifties, Gayle* was diagnosed with a chronic illness that left her semi-homebound. She'd always been a worker bee and relished practical service to her church and community. She chafed against her physical restrictions and the ensuing social isolation. She began to recognize that death was no longer an abstract, distant concept but a present reality shadowing her new normal.

Over time, Gayle's anger and frustration eventually moved her into unfamiliar territory in prayer: "Who have You made me to be in this world, Lord? Who do You want me to become as I journey with you?" She recognized that at least part of her former image as a Superstar Servant was more tied to her own need to be needed than it was to worshiping God. She recognized that God had indeed wired her to really notice the needs of others. She found new meaning in interceding for those she knew, sending notes of encouragement, and worshiping God in the small things she could still do, recognizing it was of the same value to Him as was the "widow's mite" Jesus celebrated in Luke 21:1–4.

It is rare that the discovery or affirmation of vocation at midlife is entirely disconnected from everything that came before it. God doesn't waste a thing. He redeems, and He directs our paths.

When he was in high school, Parker Palmer told everyone he wanted to be a naval aviator. His life veered away from that early goal as he moved into his college years. But later, as he reflected on that desire, he realized a clue about his true vocation as a communicator of truth had been embedded in his early career goal. Like many boys of his generation, he was fascinated with flight and spent hours building model airplanes. But unlike most of them, he also poured his energy into creating detailed illustrated booklets that explained the various parts and functions of airplanes. When he discovered a stash of those booklets decades later, he said, "I suddenly saw the truth, and it was more obvious than I had imagined. I didn't want to be a pilot or an aeronautical engineer or anything else related to aviation. I wanted to be an author, to make books—a task I have been attempting from the third grade to this very moment!"[4]

With the mirrors removed, ambitions tamped down, and the precise pruning of a Vinedresser who is fully committed to our continued growth in Him, at midlife we are in a healthy place that will allow us to better recognize what God has uniquely created us to bring to the world that He loves.

FOR INDIVIDUAL REFLECTION

1. Reflect on what the following verse tells us about vocation: "For we are God's handiwork, created in Christ Jesus to do good works, which God prepared in advance for us to do" (Eph. 2:10). What does it mean to you at this point of your life to know that you are made by God? When you consider that God has included in His creation of you a unique call you bring to the world, what questions arise for you?

2. Why do you think it is significant that Naomi's expression of bitterness in Ruth 1:20–21 is included in Scripture?

3. Author and pastor Frederick Buechner defines vocation as "the place where your deep gladness and the world's deep hunger meet."[5] Take some time to list each career aspiration, hobby, role, and job you've had throughout your life.

- Where in each of these things on your list did you experience "deep gladness"?
- Contrary to that, what about those dreams and experiences burned you out or seemed to fail?
- As you consider the needs around you, what clues does your own story give you about what God has called you to bring to the world?

FOR GROUP CONVERSATION

1. Describe the process you used to make decisions about college and/or first steps toward a career as you moved through your late teens and early twenties.

- What mirrors did you use to guide you?
- What ambitions propelled you forward?

2. Have your early career goals changed now that you've reached midlife? If so, how?

3. What brings you to tears these days? How might those tears relate to clarity about your vocation? About your congregation's sense of mission?

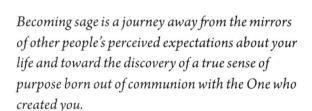

Becoming sage is a journey away from the mirrors of other people's perceived expectations about your life and toward the discovery of a true sense of purpose born out of communion with the One who created you.

CHAPTER 10

WHAT'S IT ALL ABOUT?

The wisdom of loving God and His world

For a long, long time, I moved in Christian circles where young people were coached into adulthood with motivational victory-speak that called on them to do Big Things for God. In fact, I probably used this language with an impressionable young person or two, but I'm done telling young people they're destined to turn the world upside down for Jesus. Have I gone lukewarm?

I don't think so. I've had too many heartbreaking conversations with young adult friends who eagerly responded to the ambitious "change the world" call, gave themselves over to ministry, missions, or social entrepreneurship, and then burned out after a few years in the trenches.

On the one hand, these young adults are going through coming-of-age transitions that are completely normal. But many of these crises stem from a conception of spiritual success in the church that elevates full-time Christian service and promises in so many ways that "You'll find God, save the world, and as a bonus, maybe even get some well-deserved recognition."

Young, earnest Christians in their late teens and early twenties are especially vulnerable to world changer talk as they begin to sift through vocational decisions and make choices about how to build their lives. These years are usually fueled by the ambitions and idealism that characterize Stages 2 and 3 faith, but they're a highly combustible kind of fuel. If we ignite that fuel with a one-size-fits-all, overzealous version of the Great Commission to "go into all the world," we may be lighting a rocket under young adults that launches them up, up, up with nowhere to go but down. It's painful to watch a young adult crash-land.

I've noticed that these triumphalist, world changer calls are rarely aimed at those of us in midlife and beyond. If we're maturing, ambition mellows into a search for meaning and a desire to create legacy. Even when we make dramatic life changes in our second act and move from an ambition-driven career path toward a creative or service-oriented vocation, have you noticed that the way we talk about these transitions bears little resemblance to the way we coach younger people to get out there and turn the world upside down?[1]

Author Tish Harrison Warren notes, "Maybe, at the end of days, a hurried prayer for an enemy, a passing kindness to a neighbor, or budget planning on a boring Thursday will be the revolution stories of God making all things new."[2]

God's promise of restoration to His renegade people enfolds all who belong to Him: "See, I am doing a new thing!

Now it springs up; do you not perceive it? I am making a way in the wilderness and streams in the wasteland" (Isa. 43:19). He emphasizes our present tense need for re-creation throughout Scripture up until the final movement of time in this world. "He who was seated on the throne said, 'I am making everything new!'" (Rev. 21:5).

This promise of a way in the wilderness and streams in the wasteland takes on new meaning for those of us who find our first-half-of-life ambitions have led us into the desert-like darkness that can characterize Stage 4 faith. That darkness can right-size and redirect our ambitions and help us recognize the value of living fully the life God has given us.

Mother Teresa, who spent her life serving the poorest of the poor, is often cited as the source for these powerful words: "We cannot all do great things. But we can do small things with great love."

Those words reflect the ministry God has given to each of His followers, no matter what our gifting, church affiliation, economic status, or vocation. It is the calling to what the Jewish people call *tikkun olam*, or "repairing the world." Repair means anything done to make the world a better place, from cleaning up garbage on a beach to tending the wounds of a dying AIDS patient in a Calcutta slum, as Mother Teresa did. Or it can be as small as positioning yourself at your window to wave at children walking to school each day, as 88-year-old Tinney Davidson did for twelve years straight.[3]

Lest you think this is just another way of saying "good works," we as followers of Jesus recognize that an essential way in which we participate in repairing the world is by sharing the good news of the risen Christ with those around us. That said, much of my early Christian experience was spent in church communities that focused on encouraging others to make the most important decision of their lives—praying to receive Christ as Savior and Lord. The goal was to rescue as many as possible from a godless eternity spent in hell. I learned to define myself as a follower of Jesus in terms of how effective I could be in communicating the importance of this decision to those around me. I believed that any efforts spent on this sin-sick world weren't quite as important as emphasizing life in the world to come.

Jesus never spoke or acted as if He prioritized heaven over this world. He healed, delivered, and forgave throughout His ministry so that those He'd touched would be free to serve God in this world. Consider the woman who'd been bleeding for twelve years, barred from temple worship because of her impurity (Luke 8:43–48), the demonized man who'd been exiled to live among the dead (Mark 5:1–20), or the man paralyzed who received both healing and forgiveness from Jesus (Mark 2:1–12). Each one was restored to wholeness in this world, a demonstration of the advent of His kingdom. He announced Himself at the beginning of His ministry by telling people their wait for this kingdom was over: "The time has come.... The kingdom of God has come near. Repent and believe the good news!" (Mark 1:15).

Each time Jesus healed or delivered someone, He was proclaiming the nature of His kingdom as He was returning these people to live whole and forgiven during the remainder of their time on earth. His preaching and teaching emphasized telling us what our lives would look like as we are restored to right relationship with Him. We see this illustrated most powerfully in the

Sermon on the Mount (Matt. 5–7). And after His resurrection from the dead, Jesus promised the Holy Spirit would companion and shepherd believers so they would be equipped to live as members of His kingdom here and now (John 14:15–27; 20:19–23; Acts 1:4–5).

Tikkun olam is a way in which believers live out our hope in our Savior: "The LORD will be king over the whole earth. On that day there will be one LORD, and his name the only name" (Zech. 14:9). Every act of care and kindness, no matter how small, is a way in which we as believers can express this truth.

Writer Tzvi Freeman explained, "[Tikkun olam] means that this world is not some dark, ugly place from which to escape. It is a good world; so good that as great a mess as it's become, it's still worth investing everything we've got to fix it. We believe in the Creator, so we believe in His creation . . . Tikkun provides purpose to every struggle we endure, hope for every battle we fight, destiny for every uphill journey."[4]

MAKING A LIVING OR MAKING MEANING FROM OUR LIFE

At midlife, as we shift our focus from making a living to making meaning from our lives, we can combat the feelings of disorientation we may feel in the transition by purposing to participate in kingdom-building acts of tikkun olam. I am *not* saying we can work our way out of the gloom by doing good things. But joining in God's work in repairing the world He loves can bring healing to us, too. We are part of the world in need of His repair.

The desire to create meaning from our lives grows more powerful to those becoming sage. In 1946, Holocaust survivor Victor Frankl penned a reflection on the quest for meaning. When he was imprisoned, he observed that the deeply human desire to create meaning could not be quashed even under the inhumane conditions of the camps. Frankl believed that we as human beings derive meaning from choosing courage in the face of adversity, finding value in purposeful work, and giving and receiving love.[5]

Frankl's observations wouldn't have been news to the author of Ecclesiastes. While there is some debate whether the author of the book was King Solomon or another regent, the search for meaning is echoed in the opening salvo of the book of Ecclesiastes, a book that never could have been written by a person in Stage 2 or 3 of their life. Eugene Peterson's paraphrase of these verses captures the emptiness of our human efforts to build our own kingdoms: "Smoke, nothing but smoke. . . . There's nothing to anything—it's all smoke. What's there to show for a lifetime of work, a lifetime of working your fingers to the bone?" (Eccl. 1:2, 3 MSG).

These seemingly despairing words are actually bearers of hope, as they come to us from a place that represents the recalibrated, generative faith of Stage 5. Peterson's translation of the Hebrew word *hebel* as "impermanent smoke" is usually rendered "meaningless" or "vanity." The word represents the insubstantial nature and fleeting value of the things on which we expend so much of our energy. Ecclesiastes was written by someone who tried all that the world has to offer, and found every bit of it wanting.

Author David Gibson notes that the author (whom he refers

to as the Preacher) of Ecclesiastes has a reason for his perspective on the things we use to build our lives:

> The Preacher will argue that wisdom, pleasure, work, and possessions are very often the bubbles we live in to insulate ourselves from reality. And his needle, the sharp point he uses to burst the bubbles, is death. It is the great reality facing all human beings as they go about their business on earth. Death is the one ultimate certainty that we erase from our minds and busy ourselves to avoid facing.
>
> . . . Death can radically enable us to enjoy life. By relativizing all that we do in our days under the sun, death can change us from people who want to control life for gain into people who find deep joy in receiving life as a gift. This is the main message of Ecclesiastes in a nutshell: *life in God's world is gift, not gain.*[6]

At midlife, we're confronted with the reality that death comes to us all. This existential truth can shape our quest for meaning. It is an idea Viktor Frankl would affirm.

During the period of time my mom was in hospice, an old friend reached out to me to offer support. Deborah had been a part of a church I'd had attended decades earlier. Our family moved, and Deborah and I lost touch, except for bits and pieces of news via the grapevine.

But when she called to find out how I was doing, it was as if no time had passed. She prayed for me and told me she'd love to spend some time with me when I was ready. While there was great compassion in Deborah's words, my soul detected an unexplained urgency in her tone. A few weeks after my mom's death, I called her to set a date for a get-together.

"I have cancer," she said. "I didn't want to tell you before when you were in the thick of caring for your mom during her final days."

I didn't know. My circumstances had disconnected me from the grapevine.

Despite the geographical distance that now divided us, Deborah and I were able to have a couple of deeply meaningful visits before her untimely death in her early fifties. Her illness stripped away all but what mattered most in those final months of her life. I will never forget the way she wrapped my hands in hers during our last visit. She was painfully thin, and her skin had an eerie translucent gray cast to it from the chemo. But those hands still had a surprising strength left in them. We sat together in companionable silence like that for a long time before she spoke.

"I love you."

As she faced death, nothing else really mattered. Her final months were for me a master class on what Frankl said about the quest for meaning. Deborah had always been a woman of great faith, and in the end, that faith expressed her meaning in profound ways as she lived her final days with honesty and courage, did the work of connecting with family, friends, and even a few enemies, and giving away the love she'd received from her Savior throughout her life. Frankl would have affirmed that facing death had allowed Deborah to live with meaning. I trust that the Lord simply said to her, "Well done, good and faithful servant."

It is beyond our ability to imagine what it will be like to live in union forever with the Lord—no more death, no more tears, no more suffering. We are resurrection people. But it is helpful to remember that we can't enter fully into the joy of Easter morning without first walking through the agony of Good Friday. On a lesser, human level, we cannot discover the joy of creating meaning in life without first considering death.

Perhaps it is an overflow of decision-focused faith, or perhaps it is a reflection of our culture's avoidance of the subject, but it seems that we in the church aren't always very good about talking about death. We sometimes rush to proclaim the happily-ever-after eternity in ways that can be very disorienting for those who are suffering, those who are dying, and for many of us who find ourselves at midlife having to navigate loss of all kinds.

I appreciated these words from an organization that ministers to families in the UK:

> The mission of the church in respect of bereaved people is clear. There are two specific occasions when Jesus was "moved to compassion" in the face of family grief (the stories of Lazarus and the Widow of Nain). The scriptures are full of exhortations to care for and support "widows and orphans." Overarching all is the need for the church to show Jesus' compassion and come alongside all those who are struggling and in need of support.[7]

The better we as the church get at acknowledging mortality, I believe the better we'll become at meeting those who've stumbled into the death-shadowed darkness of Stage 4 faith at midlife. By creating learning opportunities, space for lament, and honoring the memory of those who've died, we strengthen the whole body at every life stage as we affirm the reality of death even as we express our hope in the certainty of resurrection.

Learning opportunities As I noted in chapter 6, large or small group learning opportunities focused on end-of-life issues benefit everyone in the congregation. As I mentioned in chapter 6, inviting experts who serve the aged, ill, and dying to speak to your community will benefit those who attend and may well trickle down to the rest of the congregation as conversations continue among members. It also signals to all members that the church is a place that is willing to "go there" on challenging but essential issues.

Space for lament Depending on who is doing the counting, as many as 40 percent of the psalms can be classified as lament.[8] Scripture doesn't shy away from expressions of grief or confusion, but many of our congregations do. The music during our Sunday services focus on praise and celebration, which are worthy expressions of shared worship. However, it seems that we often veer away from regularly including lament in our corporate gatherings. Some leaders may be uncomfortable with the notion of injecting the "downer" of lament into the mix, but lament is worship, too. It affirms the breadth of our human condition and allows us to express our hope in God in the midst of doubt, confusion, suffering, or sorrow.

Honor memory When his wife died, one man I know asked that memorial donations be used to build a prayer garden in her name outside the church. Some older church buildings have rooms, windows, or pews with plaques noting that the physical space was given in memory of a member who'd passed. Any church, even a church without its own facility, can purpose to include the anniversary date of a member's passing on their annual calendars, using the info as a reminder to reach out to loved ones.

We in the church can be a powerful community of support around the time of a funeral, but as the event fades from corporate memory, we sometimes forget that the family and friends have the loss seared into their souls. Remembering with them is a way to grieve with those who continue to grieve as well as reminding the entire community that death is a part of our lives together. In Christ, it is not the final word, but until the end of days, it is a reality for all of us.

THE GREAT CLARIFIER

Even if our church community does a good job talking about death, it is still up to us as individuals to prayerfully work through the search to find meaning in our lives. As the writer of Ecclesiastes confronted his own mortality, he found bracing clarity about the fruitlessness of that to which he'd given his energies and the powerlessness he had over the future. He repeatedly urges his hearers to pursue wisdom even as he recognizes the temporal nature of much of it (Eccl. 1:17–18; 2:13; 7:11–12; 9:10–18). His observations emphasize that a maturing sage values wisdom as a reflection of the character of God, not because it guarantees life will get better, easier, or longer.

The Preacher exhorts us to enjoy what we can of the life God has given us (Eccl. 2:24–25; 6:3; 8:15; 11:8). This can be a way of glorifying God, and a necessary reminder for those of us at midlife who may be carrying the weight of the world on our shoulders.

As we begin to comprehend our end, the writer of Ecclesiastes exhorts us to live fully and abundantly here and now. But enjoyment of life to which he refers is not an invitation, in the words of the late Prince, to "party like it's 1999."[9] It is connected to the command to love God heart, soul, mind, and strength.

Our quest for a meaning-filled life is linked inextricably to the final words of the book: "Fear God and keep his commandments, for this is the duty of all mankind. For God will bring every deed into judgment, including every hidden thing, whether it is good or evil" (Eccl. 12:13–14). As we grow in love for God, our neighbors, and ourselves, we will become sage.

FOR INDIVIDUAL REFLECTION

1. "Any efforts spent on this sin-sick world weren't quite as important as emphasizing life in the world to come." What is your response to this observation?

2. What practices or rituals do you have for remembering family or friends who've died?

3. What makes you most uncomfortable as you ponder death? What questions do you have? What fears arise?

Pray or journal those questions and fears, and don't be too hasty to try to band-aid the discomfort by writing a quick, happy ending.

FOR GROUP CONVERSATION

1. How are the language of "world changer" and the notion of tikkun olam similar? How are they different? Which one would you say best characterizes the way in which your congregation views the world around them?

2. Is lament a regular part of your corporate worship? Why or why not?

3. How does your congregation talk about death? Commemorate death?

Becoming sage discovers meaning by seeking to both understand the temporal nature of our existence and live in light of eternity, honoring God by cooperating with Him to repair the world He made and loves.

CONCLUSION

I t may be billed as a children's book, but Margery Williams's 1922 classic *The Velveteen Rabbit* is a profound parable about midlife and beyond. If it's been a while since you read it, a quick review: A boy receives a velveteen stuffed rabbit one Christmas. The toy is soon shelved with the boy's other neglected playthings. The forgotten little rabbit's deepest longing is to become Real.

One of the most beloved passages in the book is where a fellow stuffed toy, Skin Horse, describes the process of becoming Real to the little rabbit.

> "Real isn't how you are made," said the Skin Horse. "It's a thing that happens to you. When a child loves you for a long, long time, not just to play with, but REALLY loves you, then you become Real.[1]

The Skin Horse warned the Rabbit this process would take a long, long time and require a willingness to experience hurt and decay.

The rabbit despaired. How would he ever become Real?

One day, the boy falls ill with scarlet fever, and his caregiver grabs the Rabbit off the shelf, tucking it into bed with the boy. During the boy's long convalescence, the toy becomes his best friend, growing increasingly threadbare and ragged as the months pass. At one point, the toy Rabbit spots some real rabbits at play and is disheartened to discover that he can't hop and play as the real rabbits do.

Once the boy is fully recovered, his doctor orders all the toys in his nursery to be burned. The germ-saturated, threadbare velveteen rabbit is thrown into a sack along with all the other items that are to be destroyed and left out in the garden overnight. As the toy reflects on his relationship with the boy, a real tear forms in his eye and falls to the ground. A fairy appears and carries the toy to the forest, kissing it once and telling it that because he was real to the boy, he'd now become Real to the whole world. The Rabbit discovers that his hind legs now leap and kick, and he joins the other rabbits in frolicking.

He has become Real.

ON OUR WAY TO REAL

A biographer for Margery Williams noted that her life was indelibly imprinted by the loss of her beloved father when she was just seven years old:

> The undertone of sadness and the themes of death and loss that flow through her children's books have been criticised by some reviewers, but Williams always maintained that hearts acquire greater humanity through pain and adversity.

She wrote that life is a process of constant change—there are departures for some and arrivals for others—and the process allows us to grow and persevere.[2]

At a place that exists deep within each one of us, there's an ache for an Eden we've never seen and a longing for the promise of heaven where every tear we've ever shed will be soothed away by God (Rev. 21:4). Much of our apprenticeship journey with Jesus is about trusting that He is using every bit of the pain, adversity, change, and grief of this world to transform us into the Real human beings He created us to be: "Dear friends, now we are children of God, and what we will be has not yet been made known. But we know that when Christ appears, we shall be like him, for we shall see him as he is" (1 John 3:2).

This book has focused on naming some of the key challenges we face as we seek to become sage in the second half of our lives. Midlife holds for us an invitation to move beyond the seemingly secure forms and comforting structures of faith Stages 1, 2, and 3. Believing in God, belonging to God's people, and working for God are early, foundational movements in our formation. They are as necessary to our development as crawling, then standing, then learning to walk are to the development of a runner. The progression that leads up to being able to run trains every facet of our lives—our body, certainly, but also our heart, soul, and mind. All are connected.

By refusing the invitations to move into and beyond the uncharted territory of Stage 4 faith that come disguised as often unwelcome changes in key areas of our lives, we are, in effect, pitching our tent in a faith stage we're meant to outgrow. Certainly, in His kindness, God can and does work with us if we choose to remain as crawlers instead of learning to run. But as we honor and integrate our past learning and experience and step into the darkness of Stage 4 faith, we will become free to run the rest of our life's race. As we grow toward wisdom and wholeness, we will become Real.

Which is another way of saying we are becoming sage.

HEART, SOUL, MIND, AND STRENGTH

When I was younger, I imagined a sage was someone who was a sort of living exemplar of the book of Proverbs. Sages were exceedingly ethical and always made sound decisions—wizened gray hair and hand-carved cane optional.

I've come to recognize that wisdom encompasses the beautiful moral clarity contained in the book of Proverbs, but it is so much more than that. Wisdom is no less than Jesus Himself:

> But God chose the foolish things of the world to shame the wise; God chose the weak things of the world to shame the strong. God chose the lowly things of this world and the despised things—and the things that are not—to nullify the things that are, so that no one may boast before him. It is because of him that you are in Christ Jesus, who has become for us wisdom from God—that is, our righteousness, holiness and redemption. (1 Cor 1:27–30)

We become sage

. . . in the apprenticed dailiness of seeking to love God heart, soul, mind, and strength,

. . . in our bedrooms and boardrooms,

. . . in the grief of parenting a prodigal,

... in the sorrow of losing a parent by degrees to the ravages of Alzheimer's,

... in the confusion of a church split,

... in the joy of cradling a newborn grandchild in our arms.

Though our modern tools can be helpful aids, there is no online spiritual maturity test or tidy prepackaged discipleship program that can shortcut the journey to becoming sage. Maturity is forged from the beautiful and terrible and mundane stuff of our lives as we seek to crawl, stand, walk, and run with Jesus on our way to Real.

In his article "The Major Imperatives within Mature Discipleship," author Ron Rohlheiser cited ways in which growth and spiritual progress might be observed in a follower of Jesus. His list includes ten themes, including empathy, relinquishment of envy, acceptance of suffering, forgiveness, gratitude, blessing others, increasing transparency, prayer, generous compassion, and trust.[3] We can't fully master these things in our lives; thus, they're not measurable. But the good news is that we can, sometimes with the help of others who know us well, affirm growth in these areas over time.

As we hit the "Wall" of Stage 4 and the hubris and ambitions of early adulthood begin to fade, we can begin to recognize that we are becoming the human beings God created us to be. We are free to grow into Stage 5 and 6 faith. I found that many of the items on Rohlheiser's excellent list are simply subsets of Paul's words to his friends in Corinth: "And now these three remain: faith, hope and love. But the greatest of these is love" (1 Cor 13:13). Paul understood that the process of becoming sage meant stripping away all that is not Real in our lives.

A sage is growing in faith

Our heavenly Father refines us through suffering. Author Tim Keller noted:

> Christianity teaches that, contra fatalism, suffering is overwhelming; contra Buddhism, suffering is real; contra karma, suffering is often unfair; but contra secularism, suffering is meaningful. There is a purpose to it, and if faced rightly, it can drive us like a nail deep into the love of God and into more stability and spiritual power than you can imagine.[4]

A sage lives (sometimes uncomfortably) in the tension between two seemingly disparate truths. The first is that God is neither cruel nor powerless. The second is that God is under no obligation to reveal His purposes to us. When there are no explanations, nor any relief when we are faced with suffering, we are presented with the hour-by-hour choice to trust the One who suffered for us and stands with us in our anguish.

He is not looking for triumphant heroes who deny their pain, but those who can groan Job's words from our darkness, "Though he slay me, yet will I hope in him" (Job 13:15). It may well be a battle to get to and stay in that place of trust, but the fact that we are willing to engage in that battle is an expression of maturing faith.

A fruit that grows from the excruciating pruning of suffering is empathy, sensing the emotions another may be feeling and seeking to understand their experience. A sage blesses those around them by weeping with those who weep and rejoicing with those who rejoice (Rom. 12:15), sharing the comfort they've received from God (2 Cor. 1:3–5). The process of maturity is marked by the understanding that presence *with* another who is suffering reflects faith in the One who revealed Himself to us as Immanuel (God with us) and who has promised to be with us to the end of the age (Matt. 1:22–23; 28:20).

A sage is growing in hope

With the hubris of Stages 2 and 3 drained from our lives, a sage rightly appreciates their place in the world. Not with the kind of "aw, shucks" false humility rooted in pride, but with the kind of true humility that flows from a growing understanding about their relationship to God, others, and themselves. As we grow into Stage 5 and 6 faith and continue to come to terms with our limitations, we learn to relinquish to the Lord what we may have once tried to control. Our hope in Him rightsizes our notions of who we are in this world. The process of unlearning how to perform for the approval of others leads us to discover the joy of being appropriately honest about our strengths and our weaknesses.

A humbled person is quite naturally a grateful person. While secular experts note that the cultivation of gratitude is an important practice for our mental health, as believers, we recognize that our gratitude has an object. We are not just listing the things we like about our lives but offering worship-filled thanks to the Giver of every good gift. A life steeped in thanksgiving overflows with commitment to bless others—even toward those who we may have once envied or who have acted as our enemies (Matt. 5:38–48). Hope in God is marked by humility and gratitude.

A sage is growing in love

By the time we arrive at midlife, hopefully we've discovered that true love is nothing like the lyrics of summer pop songs or the plots of Hollywood romantic comedies. A sage who is being refined in the grit of life is discovering that true love often looks just like the work and grace of forgiveness. Rohlheiser noted, "Perhaps the greatest struggle we have in the second-half of our lives is to forgive: forgive those who have hurt us, forgive ourselves for our own shortcomings, and forgive God for seemingly hanging us out unfairly to dry in this world. The greatest moral imperative of all is not to die with a bitter, unforgiving heart."[5]

Stage 5 faith (passing it on) and Stage 6 faith (heading home) are lived out of a deep understanding and experience of reconciliation to God, others, and self. He loves us heart, soul, mind, and strength. As we journey with Him, we will move toward an increasingly generous, generative life that reflects the way we are loved by Jesus: "This is how we know what love is: Jesus Christ laid down his life for us. And we ought to lay down our lives for our brothers and sisters" (1 John 3:16). As we mature, we recognize that love might look like cleaning up after a parent with dementia who has had a toileting accident . . . or holding out our arms to welcome home a prodigal child, forgiving someone who has wronged us, or passing on what we possess and what we've learned to the next generation.

Poet Robert Browning wrote:

"For life, with all it yields of joy and woe
"And hope and fear,—believe the aged friend,—
Is just our chance o' the prize of learning love."[6]

The love of one who is becoming sage looks just like the trust of a baby in a parent's arms (Ps. 131). It looks like a worn-out velveteen rabbit the night before he became Real.

It looks like Jesus.

May each one of us discover the beauty of a life apprenticed to Jesus

... bearing fruit in every season

... growing up

... growing whole

... and growing old

... becoming sage

FOR FURTHER READING

Anote from the author: Not every book on this list is written for a Christian audience, but each book included in this small selection of titles adds something to the conversation about spiritual maturity at midlife. Read with the discernment befitting a sage.

Beach, Shelly. *Ambushed by Grace: Help and Hope on the Caregiving Journey* (Grand Rapids: Discovery House Publishers, 2008).

Bourke, Dale Hanson. *Embracing Your Second Calling: Find Passion and Purpose for the Rest of Your Life* (Nashville: Thomas Nelson, 2010).

Bridges, William. *Managing Transitions: Making the Most of Change* (Cambridge, MA: Da Capo Books, 2003).

Dalfanzo, Gina. *One by One: Welcoming the Singles in Your Church* (Grand Rapids: Baker, 2017).

Dyck, Drew. *Generation Ex-Christian: Why Young Adults Are Leaving the Faith . . . and How to Bring Them Back* (Chicago: Moody, 2010).

Fowler, James. *Stages of Faith: The Psychology of Human Development and the Quest for Meaning* (New York: HarperOne, 1981).

Gibson, David. *Living Life Backward: How Ecclesiastes Teaches Us to Live in Light of the End* (Wheaton, IL: Crossway Books, 2017).

Grant, Jennifer. *When Did Everybody Else Get So Old? Indignities, Compromises, and the Unexpected Grace of Midlife* (Harrisonburg, VA: Herald Press, 2017).

Greco, Dorothy Littell. *Making Marriage Beautiful* (Colorado Springs: David C. Cook, 2018).

Hagberg, Janet and Robert Guelich. *The Critical Journey: Stages in the Life of Faith* (Salem, WI: Sheffield Publishing, 1989, 2004).

Haggerty, Barbara Bradley. *Life Reimagined: The Art, Science, and Opportunity of Midlife* (New York: Riverhead Books, 2016).

St. John of the Cross. *The Dark Night of the Soul.* You can find a free version of this book online at https://www.ccel.org/ccel/john_cross/dark_night.html. There are many inexpensive print versions of this classic, first published in the sixteenth century.

Keller, Tim. *Walking with God through Pain and Suffering* (New York: Penguin, 2013).

Lewis, C. S. *The Four Loves* (San Francisco: HarperOne, 2017).

Lewis, C. S. *A Grief Observed* (San Francisco: HarperOne, 2001).

Norris, Kathleen. *Acedia and Me: Marriage, Monks, and a Writer's Life* (New York: Riverhead Books, 2008).

Packard, Josh and Ashleigh Hope. *Church Refugees: Sociologists Reveal Why People Are DONE with Church but Not Their Faith* (Colorado Springs: Group Publishing, 2015).

Palmer, Parker. *Let Your Life Speak: Listening for the Voice of Vocation* (San Francisco: Jossey-Bass, 1999).

Rohr, Richard. *Falling Upward: A Spirituality for the Two Halves of Life* (San Francisco: Jossey-Bass 2011).

Scazzero, Peter. *Emotionally Healthy Spirituality* (Franklin, TN: Integrity, 2006).

Simpson, Amy. *Troubled Minds: Mental Illness and the Church's Mission* (Downers Grove, IL: InterVarsity Press, 2013).

ACKNOWLEDGMENTS

"As iron sharpens iron, so one person sharpens another" (Prov. 27:17). I have been sharpened through the years by a few people who have acted as my enemies. I recognize now that God has used each of them to expose my heart, challenge my soul, demand I use my mind, and marshal my strength as I've learned to follow Jesus. May God bring each one of you His shalom.

I am grateful for the gifts of many wonderful sages in my life, including my five high school BFFs, the women of the Digging Deeper Bible study, my conversation groups led by Anita Lustrea in Florida and Melinda Schmidt in Illinois, and my prayer partner of two decades, Meg Kausalik. I give thanks to God as well for the voices of the online communities of INK Creative, Her.meneutics writers group, the Pelican Project, and ThePerennialGen in my life. Each has been used by God to cultivate my faith. May He bless each one of you with His shalom too.

I benefitted greatly from the beta readers who reviewed and commented on drafts of various chapters of this book, including Pam Hill, Charm Britton, Carol Marshall, Terrie Winkates, Carole Duff, Ann and Michael Gapinski, Kate Sanderson, David Swartz, Kim Shay, Barb Best, Betty Drum, Carol Graft, Judy Allen, Melanie McGehee, Kirsten Filian, Sarah Logan, Carol Hiestand, Marcia Otting, and Joanna Whitney.

More than three years ago, Amanda Cleary Eastep and I met at a women's event. She reached out to me with an idea about a collaborative blog for midlife men and women. Those conversations led to the creation of ThePerennialGen.com—and became the basis of a wonderful, life-giving friendship. In addition to calling her my co-conspirator, I am also honored to call her my editor, as she has served in that role for my two books with Moody Publishers.

I am overflowing with gratitude to acquisitions editor Judy Dunagan and the rest of the team at Moody. You guys have made my work better and put forth incredible, creative effort in connecting that work with readers. Thanks, too, to agents Dan Balow and Steve Laube, who have cheered me on and advocated for me.

Thankfully, forty years ago, my husband, Bill, decided to ignore the counsel of that person who called me the pinnacle of immaturity. We've been together since then, for better, for worse, for richer, for poorer, in sickness, and in health. I am glad I got to grow up with you, Bill. I love you.

My children and grandchildren have been some of my most important teachers. Loving you and watching each one of you grow up has been a high honor. I cherish each one of you and pray that you will each sink your roots into the width, length, height, and depth of the love your Savior has for you (Eph. 3:18). This is the essence of a sage, well-lived life.

I am humbled and grateful for each of you reading this book. May this promise be your compass as you journey toward teleios: ". . . he who began a good work in you will carry it on to completion until the day of Christ Jesus" (Phil. 1:6).

My Lord, I thank You for Your pure compassion and perfect love. Your mercies are indeed new every single morning, and Your faithfulness is beyond measure.

NOTES

Introduction

1. "teleios," The KJV New Testament Greek Lexicon, Bible Study Tools, https://www.biblestudytools.com/lexicons/greek/kjv/teleios.html.
2. R. Kent Hughes, "4 Essentials for Spiritual Maturity," Ligonier Ministries, July 17, 2017, https://www.ligonier.org/blog/4-essentials-spiritual-maturity.
3. Lindsay M. Howden and Julie A. Meyer, "Age and Sex Composition: 2010," U.S. Census Bureau, issued May, 2011, https://www.census.gov/prod/cen2010/briefs/c2010br-03.pdf. Becky Gillan, "Top 10 Demographics & Interests Facts about Americans Age 50+," May 14, 2014, http://blog.aarp.org/2014/05/14/top-10-demographics-interests-facts-about-americans-age-50/.
4. Barna Group, "Barna Describes Religious Changes Among Busters, Boomers, and Elders Since 1991," July 26, 2011, https://www.barna.com/research/barna-describes-religious-changes-among-busters-boomers-and-elders-since-1991. Michelle Van Loon, "The Midlife Church Crisis," *Christianity Today*, September 3, 2014, https://www.christianitytoday.com/ct/2014/september/midlife-church-crisis.html.

Chapter 1: Grow Up!

1. Spiritual Maturity Assessment, Fellowship of Companies for Christ International, https://fcci.org/assessments/spiritual-maturity-assessment.
2. Barna Group, "Many Churchgoers and Faith Leaders Struggle to Define Spiritual Maturity," May 11, 2009, https://www.barna.com/research/many-churchgoers-and-faith-leaders-struggle-to-define-spiritual-maturity/.
3. Ibid.
4. Aaron Buer, "3 Ways We Measure Spiritual Growth," Breeze, February 23, 2017, https://www.breezechms.com/blog/3-ways-we-measure-spiritual-growth/.
5. William T. Ellis, *Billy Sunday: The Man and His Message* (Philadelphia: John C. Winston Publishing, 1917), 155.
6. Jan Johnson, "Living as an Apprentice to the Master," excerpted from *Discipleship Journal*, Issue 107, September 1998, published December 4, 2017 on https://www.navigators.org/living-as-an-apprentice-to-the-master/.
7. First Corinthians 13:11; Ephesians 4:13–15; Hebrews 5:13–14.
8. J. Oswald Sanders, *Cultivation of Christian Character* (Chicago, IL: Moody, 1965), 11.
9. John 15:13; Galatians 2:20; Acts 1:8; 2 Peter 1:3–4:4.
10. Galatians 5:22–23; Colossians 1:9–14; Job 28:28; 1 Corinthians 1:30.

Chapter 2: Midlife and Beyond

1. Richard Rohr, *Falling Upward: A Spirituality for the Two Halves of Life* (San Francisco: Jossey-Bass, 2011), Kindle edition, 225, 270.
2. "1900–2000: Changes In Life Expectancy in the United States," SeniorLiving .org, https://www.seniorliving.org/history/1900-2000-changes -life-expectancy-united-states.
3. The Who, "My Generation" (1965), https://www.youtube.com/watch? v=qN5zw04WxCc.
4. Reveal for Church, https://revealforchurch.com/; "What *Reveal* Reveals," *Christianity Today*, February 27, 2008, https://www.christianitytoday.com/ ct/2008/march/11.27.html.
5. James Fowler, *Stages of Faith: The Psychology of Human Development and the Quest for Meaning* (New York: HarperOne, 1981).
6. Janet Hagberg and Robert Guelich, *The Critical Journey: Stages in the Life of Faith* (Salem, WI: Sheffield Publishing, 1989, 2004).
7. Ibid., 73.
8. Scholars can't accurately date how long David was on the run: Lee Woofenden, "How long was David on the run from Saul?," *Stack Exchange: Christianity*, October 22, 2017, https://christianity.stackexchange.com/questions/52930/ how-long-was-david-on-the-run-from-saul.
9. Madeleine L'Engle, *The Crosswicks Journal: A Circle of Quiet* (New York: Farrar, Straus and Giroux, 1971), 113.
10. Janet Hagberg and Robert Guelich, *The Critical Journey*, 115.
11. Second Samuel 7:16.
12. Steve Stockman, *Walk On: The Spiritual Journey of U2* (Orlando, FL: Relevant Books, 2012), 74.

Chapter 3: Going to Church, Being the Church

1. Michelle Van Loon, "Over 40? Share Your Church Experience via Brief Survey," Patheos.com, April 18, 2013, https://www.patheos.com/blogs/ pilgrims roadtrip/2013/04/over-40-share-your-church-experience-survey.
2. This section of the book summarizes my 2013 blog series. The final in the series also appeared on Patheos: "40+ and the Church/Survey Final," May 27, 2013, Patheos.com, https://www.patheos.com/blogs/pilgrimsroad trip/2013/05/40-and-the-church-survey-final.
3. Amy Simpson, "Should Churches Stop Asking for Volunteers?," AmySimpson.com April 10, 2012, http://amysimpson.com/2012/04/ should-churches-stop-asking-for-volunteers/.
4. U.S. Census Bureau, "Unmarried and Single Americans Week 2017," August 14, 2017, https://www.census.gov/content/dam/Census/newsroom/facts- for-features/2017/cb17-ff16.pdf.

5. Josh Packard and Ashleigh Hope, *Church Refugees: Sociologists Reveal Why People Are DONE with Church but Not Their Faith* (Colorado Springs: Group Publishing, 2015).

6. W. Robertson Nicoll, ed. *The Expositor's Greek New Testament* (Grand Rapids: Eerdmans Publishing, 1956). From the *Expositor's Greek New Testament*, highlighted here: https://www.preceptaustin.org/hebrews_1024-25.

Chapter 4: We Heart Family

1. Posted by Margaret Hunter, "How Long Was Joseph In Potiphar's House? How Long In Prison?", Amazing Bible Timeline, June 29, 2013, https://amazingbibletimeline.com/blog/q27_joseph_how_long_in_prison/.

2. Many quote-gathering sites attribute this line to George Bernard Shaw. https://www.google.com/search?q=A+happy+family+is+but+an+earlier+heaven.+George+Bernard+Shaw&rlz=1C5CHFA_enUS512US512&ei=xMttXLbUOMfisAW2rKPYDw&start=0&sa=N&ved=0ahUKEwi2xpbUpcvgAhVHMawKHTbWCPs4ChDy0wMIbQ&biw=782&bih=432. However, Goodreads attributes it to author and politician John Bowring: https://www.goodreads.com/quotes/315741-a-happy-family-is-but-an-earlier-heaven.

3. Jonathan Edwards, *The Works of Jonathan Edwards*, vol. 2 (London: William Ball, 1839), 244.

4. Concept taken from: William Bridges, *Managing Transitions: Making the Most of Change* (Cambridge, MA: Da Capo Books, 2003), 28–29.

5. Susan L. Brown, I-Fen Lin, and Krista K. Payne, "Age Variation in the Divorce Rate, 1990-2012," nd, National Center for Family and Marriage Research at Bowling Green State University, https://www.bgsu.edu/content/dam/BGSU/college-of-arts-and-sciences/NCFMR/documents/FP/FP-14-16-age-variation-divorce.pdf.

6. "Evangelicals Have Higher-than-Average Divorce Rates, according to a Report Compiled by Baylor for the Council on Contemporary Families," Baylor University Media and Public Relations, February 5, 2014, https://www.baylor.edu/mediacommunications/news.php?action=story&story=137892. Sarah Zylstra, "Are Evangelicals Bad for Marriage?," *Christianity Today*, February 14, 2014, https://www.christianitytoday.com/ct/2014/february-web-only/are-evangelicals-bad-for-marriage.html; "U.S. divorce rates: for various faith groups, age groups, and geographical areas," Religious Tolerance, July 20, 2009, https://www.religioustolerance.org/chr_dira.htm.

7. Vivian Diller, "'Til Gray Do We Part: Can Marriage Survive Midlife," PsychologyToday.com, May 17, 2011, https://www.psychologytoday.com/us/blog/face-it/201105/til-gray-do-we-part-can-marriage-survive-midlife.

8. Belinda Luscombe, "Why Even the Best Marriages Are Hard Sometimes," Time.com, January 26, 2018, http://time.com/5117440/great-marriage-hard/.

9. Christina Ianzito, "Elder Orphans: How to Plan for Aging Without a Family Caregiver," AARP.com, December 13, 2016, https://www.aarp.org/caregiving/basics/info-2017/tips-aging-alone.html.

10. Connie Gochenaur, "Sacrifice, Surrender, and Survival," ThePerennialGen.com, May 4, 2018, https://theperennialgen.com/sacrifice-surrender-and-survival/.

11. Robin Marantz Henig, "The Age of Grandparents Is Made of Many Tragedies," TheAtlantic.com, June 1, 2018, https://www.theatlantic.com/family/archive/2018/06/this-is-the-age-of-grandparents/561527/.

12. C. S. Lewis, *A Grief Observed* (San Francisco: HarperOne, 2001), 11.

13. Jamie Janosz, "Breathe In. Breathe Out.", ThePerennialGen.com, August 1, 2017, https://theperennialgen.com/breathe-in-breathe-out/.

14. Drew Dyck, *Generation Ex-Christian: Why Young Adults Are Leaving the Faith . . . and How to Bring Them Back* (Chicago: Moody, 2010), Kindle edition, 220.

15. Ibid., location 540.

16. Ibid., location 825–26.

17. Ibid., location 1243.

18. Ibid., location 1548.

19. Ibid., location 1829.

20. Bill Mounce, "Aktionsart and Ask, Seek, Knock (Matt 7:7–8)," BillMounce.com, May 22, 2017, https://www.billmounce.com/monday-with-mounce/aktionsart-and-ask-seek-knock-matt-7-7-8.

21. "Giving Thanks Can Make You Happier," Healthbeat, Harvard Health Publishing, https://www.health.harvard.edu/healthbeat/giving-thanks-can-make-you-happier.

Chapter 5: Forever Friends

1. The preceding three paragraphs were adapted from my article "Why Friends Disappear When You Reach Midlife," *Christianity Today*, August 2012, https://www.christianitytoday.com/women/2012/august/why-friends-disappear-when-you-reach-midlife.html.

2. Thomas Aquinas, *Summa Theologica*, vol. 2 (New York: Cosimo Book, 2007).

3. C. S. Lewis, *The Four Loves* (San Francisco: HarperOne, 2017), 114.

4. Janet Adamy and Paul Overberg, "The Loneliest Generation: Americans, More Than Ever, Are Aging Alone," https://www.wsj.com/articles/the-loneliest-generation-americans-more-than-ever-are-aging-alone-11544541134.

5. "Aging Alone," Wall Street Journal, December 11, 2018, https://jamanetwork.com/journals/jamainternalmedicine/fullarticle/1188033, *Wall Street Journal*, December 11, 2018.

6. Barbara Bradley Haggerty, *Life Reimagined: The Science, Art, and Opportunity of Midlife* (New York: Riverhead Books, 2016), 108.

7. Henri Nouwen, "From Loneliness to Solitude," Henri Nouwen Society, February 8, 2019, https://henrinouwen.org/meditation/from-loneliness -to-solitude/.

8. "5 Camp Songs Every Girl Scout Should Know, GSblog, July 25, 2015, https: //blog.girlscouts.org/2015/07/5-camp-songs-every-girl-scout-should.html.

9. The preceding three paragraphs adapted from my article "Don't Let Women's Ministry Turn People into Projects," *Christianity Today*, June 2013, https:// www.christianitytoday.com/women/2013/june/dont-let-womens-ministry -turn-people-into-projects.html.

Chapter 6: Glorify God with *This* Body?

1. Melissa Conrad Stöppler, "What Should You Know about Menopause?", nd, https://www.emedicinehealth.com/menopause/article_em.htm.

2. "Perimenopause," nd, WebMD.com, https://www.webmd.com/menopause/ guide/guide-perimenopause#.

3. "Man Fully Alive Is the Glory of God—Irenaeus," Crossroadsinitiative.com, https://www.crossroadsinitiative.com/media/articles/man-fully-alive-is-the-glory-of-god-st-irenaeus/, Crossroadsinitiative.com.

4. N. T. Wright, "Mind, Spirit, Soul and Body: All for One and One for All Reflections on Paul's Anthropology in his Complex Contexts," NTWright-page.com, March 18, 2011, http://ntwrightpage.com/2016/07/12/mind -spirit-soul-and-body/.

5. David Briggs, "This Is My Body: How Christian Theology Affects Body Image," *Christianity Today*, October 26, 2016, https://www.christianitytoday.com/ news/2016/october/how-christian-theology-affects-body-image-body-shaming.html.

6. Correspondence from Barb Best.

7. James B. Nelson and Sandra P. Longfellow, eds., *Sexuality and the Sacred: Sources for Theological Reflection* (Louisville, KY: Westminster John Knox Press, 1994), 234.

8. Alexa Lardieri, "Study: Many Adults Ages 65 to 80 Continue to Be Sexu-ally Active," *U.S. News*, May 3, 2018, https://www.usnews.com/news/ health-care-news/articles/2018-05-03/study-many-adults-ages-65-to-80-continue-to-be-sexually-active.

9. The previous two paragraphs were adapted from my article "Sex, Drugs, and Getting Old," *Christianity Today*, June 2015, https://www.christianitytoday .com/women/2015/june/sex-drugs-and-getting-old.html.

10. Adapted from my article "We Don't Age Out of Our Sexuality," *Christianity Today*, February 2016, https://www.christianitytoday.com/women/2016/ february/we-dont-age-out-of-our-sexuality.html?start=1.

11. Margaret Kim Peterson and Dwight Peterson, *Are You Waiting for "The One"?*: *Cultivating Realistic, Positive Expectations for Christian Marriage* (Downers Grove, IL: InterVarsity Press, 2011), 27.

12. Claire Ansberry, "What Is the Perfect Age?," *Wall Street Journal*, January 13, 2018, https://www.wsj.com/articles/what-is-the-perfect-age-1515844860.

13. Vivian Diller and Jill Muir-Sukenick, "Why Smart Women Still Agonize Over Aging," Today.com, March 10, 2010, https://www.today.com/popculture/why-smart-women-still-agonize-over-aging-wbna35803098.

14. Lindsay Cook, "Ageism in the Workplace 'Starts at 40' for Women," *Financial Times*, December 21, 2018, https://www.ft.com/content/e4141576-04eb-11e9-99df-6183d3002ee1.

15. Cynthia McFadden and Mary Marsh, "How Joyce Meyer Built a Worldwide Following," ABCnews.go.com, April 13, 2010, https://abcnews.go.com/Nightline/joyce-meyer-transparent-evangelist/story?id=10355887&page=2.

16. Shelly Beach, "Cosmetic Surgery to the Glory of God?", *Christianity Today*, April 7, 2010, https://www.christianitytoday.com/women/2010/april/cosmetic-surgery-to-glory-of-god.html.

17. Asked 3/2/19 on both my personal page and on ThePerennialGen.com Facebook page.

18. Sarah Elizabeth Adler, "Heart Disease Deaths Rise for U.S. Adults, CDC Says," AARP, May 23, 2019, https://www.aarp.org/health/conditions-treatments/info-2019/heart-disease-cancer-death-rates.html.

Chapter 7: You Can't Take It with You

1. Jacques Ellul, *Money and Power* (Eugene, OR: Wipf & Stock Publishers, 1984), 75–76.

2. Brandon Peach, "The 'American Dream' Isn't the Goal of the Christian Life," *Relevant*, October 10, 2017, https://relevantmagazine.com/article/the-american-dream-isnt-the-goal-of-the-christian-life.

3. History.com Editors, "FDIC," History.com, August 3, 2017, https://www.history.com/topics/great-depression/history-of-the-fdic.

4. Viktoria Ney, "Many Americans Ended Up Homeless during the Real Estate Crisis 10 Years Ago— Here's Where They Are Now," Business Insider, August 7, 2018, https://www.businessinsider.com/heres-where-those-who-lost-homes-during-the-us-housing-crisis-are-now-2018-8.

5. Amy Medina, "God Doesn't Owe Me The American Dream", June 24, 2016, https://gilandamy.blogspot.com/2016/06/god-doesnt-owe-me-american-dream.html, Everyone Needs A Little Grace In Their Lives/gilandamyblogspot.

6. A slightly shorter version of this account is also found in Luke 21:1–4.

7. https://www.biblestudytools.com/dictionaries/bakers-evangelical-dictionary/widow.html.

8. Juliana LaBianca, "These People Donated Millions After They Died—But No One Knew They Were Rich," *Reader's Digest*, https://www.rd.com/true-stories/inspiring/secret-millionaires-donations-after-died/.

9. Lisa Schmeiser, "Why Are Millennials Rejecting Prized Family Possessions?," August 23, 2017, https://observer.com/2017/08/millennials-rejecting-baby-boomer-family-possessions-marie-kondo-experience-economy, *Observer*.

Chapter 8: Happiness Is Spelled with a "U"

1. Christopher Ingraham, "Under 50? You Still Haven't Hit Rock Bottom, Happiness-wise," August 24, 2017, *Washington Post*, https://www.washingtonpost.com/news/wonk/wp/2017/08/24/under-50-you-still-havent-hit-rock-bottom-happiness-wise/?noredirect=on&utm_term=.ef765758fa78.

2. Barbara Bradley Haggerty, *Life Reimagined: The Science, Art, and Opportunity of Midlife* (New York: Riverhead Books, 2016), 27–28.

3. Kathleen Fifield, "Suicide Deaths Are Up Sharply, CDC Says," AARP.com, https://www.aarp.org/health/conditions-treatments/info-2018/suicide-up-among-older-americans.html; Deborah M. Stone, Thomas R. Simon, Katherine A. Fowler et al., "*Vital Signs*: Trends in State Suicide Rates—United States, 1999–2016 and Circumstances Contributing to Suicide—27 States, 2015," Centers for Disease Control and Prevention, June 8, 2018, https://www.cdc.gov/mmwr/volumes/67/wr/mm6722a1.htm, Centers for Disease Control and Prevention, June 8, 2018.

4. "Depression," National Institute of Mental Health, https://www.nimh.nih.gov/health/topics/depression/index.shtml, nd.

5. Ibid.

6. Jenna Baddeley, "Depression and its metaphors," November 3, 2008, https://www.psychologytoday.com/us/blog/embracing-the-dark-side/200811/depression-and-its-metaphors, *Psychology Today,*

7. Paul E. Greenberg, "The Growing Economic Burden of Depression in the U.S.," *MIND Guest Blog, Scientific American*, February 25, 2015, https://blogs.scientificamerican.com/mind-guest-blog/the-growing-economic-burden-of-depression-in-the-u-s/.

8. Kay Warren's resources for local churches can be accessed here: kaywarren.com/mentalhealth. Writer and speaker Amy Simpson's 2013 book *Troubled Minds: Mental Illness and the Church's Mission* is essential reading on the topic. NAMI FaithNet's online home is nami.org/Get-Involved/NAMI-FaithNet.

9. "Acedia (or Sloth)," Paths of Love, 2018, https://www.pathsoflove.com/acedia/acedia.html.

10. Kathleen Norris, *Acedia & Me: A Marriage, Monks, and a Writer's Life* (New York: Riverhead Books, 2008), 3, 200.

11. Ibid., 200.

12. This theological error is known as *dualism*: "The theory that the universe has been ruled from its origins by two conflicting powers, one good and one evil, both existing as equally ultimate first causes" (The Free Dictionary, s.v. "dualism," https://www.thefreedictionary.com/dualism, *Collins English Dictionary – Complete and Unabridged*, 12th ed. [New York: HarperCollins, 2014]).

13. Exodus 20:3; Psalm 86:10; Isaiah 44:6–8; Isaiah 45:5–6; John 8:58; Colossians 1:16; Jude 24–25

14. Peter Scazzero, *Emotionally Healthy Spirituality* (Franklin, TN: Integrity Publishers, 2006), 44–46.

15. Peter Scazzero, *Emotionally Healthy Spirituality: Unleash a Revolution in Your Life In Christ* (Grand Rapids: Zondervan, 2017), 19.

Chapter 9: From Doing to Being

1. Parker Palmer, *Let Your Life Speak: Listening for the Voice of Vocation* (San Francisco: Jossey-Bass, 1999), 3.

2. Janet Hagberg and Robert Guelich, *The Critical Journey: Stages in the Life of Faith* (Salem, WI: Sheffield Publishing, 1989), 109.

3. Frederick Buechner, *A Crazy, Holy Grace: The Healing Power of Pain and Memory* (Grand Rapids: Zondervan, 2017), 124–25.

4. Parker Palmer, *Let Your Life Speak*, 15.

5. "Vocation," Frederick Buechner, July 18, 2017, https://www.frederickbuechner.com/quote-of-the-day/2017/7/18/vocation.

Chapter 10: What's It All About?

1. The preceding paragraphs adapted from my article "Why I'm Not a World Changer," *Christianity Today*, August 19, 2016, https://www.christianitytoday.com/women/2016/august/why-im-not-world-changer.html.

2. Tish Harrison Warren, "Courage in the Ordinary," *The Well*, April 3, 2013, http://thewell.intervarsity.org/blog/courage-ordinary.

3. Caitlin Keating, "Woman, 88, Has Been Waving from Her Window for 12 Years—Now 400 Kids Give Their Final Goodbye," People.com, April 30, 2019, https://people.com/human-interest/tinney-davidson-final-wave-goodbye-children.

4. Tzvi Freeman, "Tikkun Olam: A Brief History," Chabad.org., https://www.chabad.org/library/article_cdo/aid/2614791/jewish/Tikkun-Olam-A-Brief-History.htm.

5. Maria Popova, "Viktor Frankl and the Human Search for Meaning," Brain Pickings, March 26, 2013, https://www.brainpickings.org/2013/03/26/viktor-frankl-mans-search-for-meaning.

6. David Gibson, *Living Life Backward: How Ecclesiastes Teaches Us to Live in Light of the End* (Wheaton, IL: Crossway Books, 2017), 37.

7. "Bereavement and the church," careforthefamily.org.uk, https://www.care forthefamily.org.uk/family-life/bereavement-support/supporting-bereaved -people/bereavement-and-the-church.

8. Richard Beck, "Not Learning to Lament: Comparing the Psalms to Songbooks," Experimental Theology, November 14, 2012, experimentaltheology.blogspot .com/2012/11/not-learning-to-lament-comparing-psalms.html; Dennis Bratcher, "Types of Psalms, Classifying the Psalms by Genre," The Voice, 2018, http://www.crivoice.org/psalmtypes.html.

9. The song "1999" is found on the 1982 album of the same name, released by Prince on the Warner Brothers label.

Conclusion

1. Margery Williams, *The Velveteen Rabbit* (New York: Doubleday, 1991) 17.

2. "Margery Williams," Poemhunter.com, https://www.poemhunter.com/ margery-williams/biography.

3. Ron Rohlheiser, "The Major Imperatives within Mature Discipleship," Transforming Center, November 16, 2018, https://transformingcenter .org/2018/11/the-major-imperatives-within-mature-discipleship.

4. Timothy Keller, *Walking with God through Pain and Suffering* (New York: Penguin, 2013), 30.

5. Rohlheiser, "The Major Imperatives within Mature Discipleship."

6. Robert Browning, "A Death in the Desert," Poetry Foundation, https:// www.poetryfoundation.org/poems/43752/a-death-in-the-desert-56d222942c57c.

Why are we so restless?

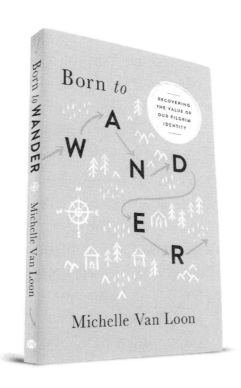

Born to Wander is about defining and embracing our biblical call to pilgrimage. Weaving together personal stories with keen insights on the themes of pilgrimage and exile in Scripture, Michelle Van Loon will help you understand and own your pilgrim identity, reorienting your heart to the God who leads you home.

978-0-8024-1812-8 | also available as eBook and audiobook

That wasn't a white hair, was it?

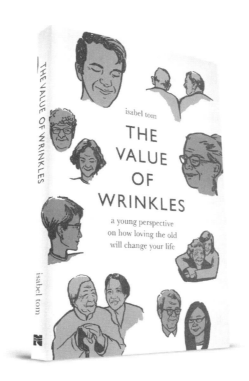